# THE REFRACTIVE THINKER®

AN ANTHOLOGY OF
DOCTORAL WRITERS

VOLUME XXIII
## Criminal Justice
### Effective Ethical Policies & Practices

Edited by Dr. Cheryl A. Lentz

THE REFRACTIVE THINKER® PRESS

*The Refractive Thinker®: An Anthology of Higher Learning*
*Vol. XXIII: Criminal Justice: Effective Ethical Policies & Practices*

**The Refractive Thinker® Press**
https://refractivethinker.com
https://Twitter.com/DrCherylLentz
https://www.Facebook.com/RefractiveThinker

The Refractive Thinker® is a registered trademark of The Lentz Leadership Institute LLC.

All rights reserved. No part of this book may be reproduced or transmitted in any form or by any means, graphic, electronic or mechanical, including photocopying, recording, taping, Web distribution, or by any informational storage and retrieval system without written permission from the publisher except for the inclusion of brief quotations in a review or scholarly reference.

Books are available through The Refractive Thinker® Press at special discounts for bulk purchases for the purpose of sales promotion, seminar attendance, or educational purposes. Special volumes can be created for specific purposes and to organizational specifications. Please contact us for further details.

*Individual authors own the copyright to their individual materials.*
*The Refractive Thinker® Press has each author's permission to reprint.*

Copyright © 2023 by The Refractive Thinker® Press
Managing Editor: Dr. Cheryl A. Lentz • DrCherylLentz@gmail.com

ISBN: 978-1-7376538-8-2

Library of Congress Control Number: 2013945437

*Kindle and electronic versions available

Refractive Thinker® logo by Joey Root; The Refractive Thinker® Press logo design by Jacqueline Teng; cover design and production by Gary A. Rosenberg.

# Contents

Testimonials, v

Foreword by Dr. Wendy Patrick, JD, MDiv, PhD, xi

Preface, xv

Acknowledgments, xix

### CHAPTER 1
Sustaining Small Businesses Through Criminal Justice and Employee Retention, 1
**Dr. Anastasia Persad & Dr. JaQuane Jones**

### CHAPTER 2
Effective Strategies to Reduce Data Breach in Hospitals, 19
**Dr. Frank Musmar**

### CHAPTER 3
The Effect of Ethical Leadership on Employee Engagement: A Moral Approach to Management, 39
**Dr. Kevin Grant**

### CHAPTER 4
Smoke and Mirrors—The Illusion of Education in America's Schools: Compulsory Preparation for Incarceration, 55
**Dr. Teresa Sanders**

CHAPTER 5

Leaders in American Institutions: Affecting Change for Diversity, Equity, and Inclusion, 73

**Dr. Anita A. Francis & Dr. Paula Schuh Berbeco**

CHAPTER 6

A Solution to the Labor Shortage: Reformed Offenders Could be the Answer, 91

**Dr. Karen Balcanoff, Dr. Judie Brill, Dr. Wendy J. Mizerek-Herrburger, & Dr. James Wright**

CHAPTER 7

Educate or Litigate? The Mindsets of Advancing Knowledge and Maintaining Financial Stability in Higher Education, 111

**Dr. Cherri Brown & Dr. Cheryl Lentz**

Index, 129

2023 Catalog, 131

# Testimonials

### Brian Jud

Executive Director of the Association of Publishers for Special Sales, author of 14 books including *How to Make Real Money Selling Books* (2nd Edition) http://www.bookmarketingworks.com/

Authors always want to know the latest out-of-the-box strategy to sell more of their books. *The Refractive Thinker*® series adopts this innovative-thinking approach, so you can get your doctoral research out of academia and into the hands of those who need it. This volume, specific to the field of work-life balance is a particularly good example of how to make that happen regarding strategies to enhance workflow and productivity. There is no need to go it alone. Join your colleagues on a journey in search of innovative solutions as you navigate the landscape of business.

### Clarissa Burt

CEO/Founder of *In the Limelight*
https://clarissaburt.com/
https://clarissaburt.com/magazine/

Learning doesn't always happen in a formal classroom; sometimes one learns from the school of hard knocks and experience. *The Refractive Thinker*® series looks to connecting these two worlds of business and learning in this volume regarding work-life balance—the ability to focus on strategies for effective personal and professional outcomes. A refractive thinker® is one who never settles for anything less than everything, daring to question what is, in favor of what might be. Dr. Cheryl Lentz dared to change the model of academic publishing by understanding the power of connection between education and business—to make research more accessible to business owners and entrepreneurs. No one benefits from playing small, particularly with one's personal passion in the world of knowledge. Refractive thinkers play on a big stage, truly desiring to change their world and ours. Join them.

### Mark James

Business speaker; President/Founder, Performance Advisors Group, Inc. Delivering results that count, that can be counted for B2B companies. https://www.linkedin.com/in/performadvisors

The journey to success, personally and professionally, is rarely without barriers or twists in the road. As the name implies, *The Refractive Thinker*® series is an excellent source of knowledge to help you change direction through barriers to overcome them and proceed onward to your goals. And this book will be an invaluable companion to your work-life journey.

# Testimonials

## Abby E. Gooch, C.E.O., Life Force Connection

Author, Speaker, Intuitive Success Coach
*Success From The Inside Out!*
success@lifeforceconnection.com
www.lifeforceconnection.com
www.oneheartglobal.com

Dr. Cheryl Lentz is a beautiful soul full of integrity and love. I feel so blessed to have had her guest as a guest on *Oneness Talk* radio and I know anyone who comes across her path will be blessed! Be sure to review the wisdom offered by her and these scholars regarding the importance of work-life balance for your life.

## Phyllis Ayman, MS/SLP, CDP, CADDCT, CMDCP

*Ambassador for Conscious Aging Life Management*
CEO, Phyllis Ayman Associates
#1 *WSJ* and *USA Today* Bestselling Author
UN NGO Committee on Aging
U.S. Eastern Region Chair - G 100
Babyboomer.org expert
www.phyllisaymanassociates.com

Dr. Cheryl Lentz in this all-important series *The Refractive Thinker*® understands the critically important intersection of critical thinking and experience. She applies the social theories of Paolo Friere to the concept that education is an important element in the citizen's connection to community. In doing so, Dr. Cheryl brings together her extraordinary education and expertise with fellow thought leaders and educators, to examine and find solutions to some of some of our most important societal business, social and political dilemmas.

This critical work is a must-read for all who believe, want to seek and understand the possibilities for changing how our society functions. I can personally attest to the resulting neglect, inadequate care, and substandard quality of life for those entrusted to the care of the system as well as the treatment of the workforce who cares for them. From there, each chapter unveils the opportunity for us to apply our highest order of thinking and intellect through one lens to broaden our perspective, guide our thinking and hopefully inspire our advocacy to hopefully make needed changes across several sectors.

*"Injustice anywhere is a threat to justice everywhere. We are caught in an inescapable network of mutuality, tied in a single garment of destiny. Whatever affects one directly, affects all indirectly."*

—Martin Luther King, Jr.

*"Justice will not be served until those who are unaffected are as outraged as those who are."*

—Benjamin Franklin

# Foreword

### Dr. Wendy Patrick, JD, MDiv, PhD

Life presents challenges in how we learn to see people in our lives. While we all need emotional blinders at times, the questions to ask are how we can protect those around us—our family, our friends, our coworkers—to spot deceptive or downright dangerous people to find a safer way forward. Blinded by desire from the allure of positive attention, we can miss important details. We overlook red flags that can prevent us from distinguishing the dangerous from the desirable, from sexual predators to financial manipulators, to domestic abusers. The goal is to learn how to correctly read people through situational awareness, verifying information, and noting inconsistencies. How do you truly distinguish between friend or frenemy? How can you "hear between the lines" to detect a lie? And what do you do when realization hits that not everyone is who you think they are?

Through my decades of experience, corroborated by empirical research, the goal is to pay close attention and learn how to spot critical clues, both personally and professionally, that will enable you to perceive trustworthiness and integrity. We must guard our feelings and not be seduced by the selective attention of charmers, manipulators, and those who have mastered the art of deceit. These wolves in sheep's clothing can deceive us through generating emotional intoxication which can mute the sharp colors of the red flags they are flying. Whether your focus is friendship or marriage, career or family, romance or professional success, accurately reading people and perceiving signs of danger enables you to trade your rose colored glasses for reading glasses.

Using relatable, real-life examples, my experiences will help you assess people and circumstances clearly and accurately, identify healthy sources of attraction, to surround yourself with trustworthy, safe, compassionate people.

Dr. Cheryl Lentz and contributing scholars in this latest edition of *The Refractive Thinker*® series add their lessons learned from their doctoral level research and their experience and wisdom on how to navigate people and circumstances in the Criminal Justice System using a variety of lenses in business, the community, and the halls of academia. Their stories and reflections will provide additional insights on how to move forward effectively. I recommend you listen closely.

Dr. Wendy Patrick
http://WendyPatrickphd.com

## About the Author...

**Dr. Wendy L. Patrick** is a career prosecutor, named the Ronald M. George Public Lawyer of the Year by the California State Bar's Public Law Section. She has been recognized by her peers as one of the Top Ten criminal attorneys in San Diego by the *San Diego Daily Transcript*.

Dr. Patrick has completed over 160 trials ranging from hate crimes to domestic violence, to first-degree murder. Much of her career has been spent prosecuting domestic abusers, sexually violent predators, human traffickers, stalkers, rapists, and child molesters. She has spent over 26 years lecturing and speaking both domestically and internationally on the topics of sexual assault, domestic violence, threat assessment, and human trafficking, which she has taught in Hong Kong, South Africa, and South Korea. She teaches sexual assault prevention for several branches of the United States military, including the Navy, the Air Force, and the United States Army, both domestically and internationally.

Dr. Patrick's doctoral thesis focused on the psychology of attraction used by sexual predators to ingratiate themselves with victims and their families, focusing on what can be learned from the science of seduction. She has been involved with the San Diego Sexual Assault Response Team, from whom she received the SART Response with a Heart Award for her significant contribution to the professional field of sexual assault prosecution.

As a private consultant, Dr. Wendy researches, publishes, and trains extensively on topics related to interpersonal violence, sexual assault, and working with victims to a wide variety of educational, community, and law enforcement groups. She also serves as a trial consultant and expert witness in the area of sexual assault dynamics between perpetrators and victims, and all other areas of victimology.

To reach **Dr. Wendy Patrick** for information regarding Black Swan Verdicts, Threat Assessment and Consulting, or guest speaking, please visit her **website:** http://WendyPatrickphd.com or **e-mail:** jstcesq@live.com

# Preface

Welcome to the award winning Refractive Thinker® doctoral anthology series. We are thrilled to have you join us for the 23rd volume in the series, *The Refractive Thinker® Vol XXIII: Criminal Justice.* Join us as we continue to celebrate the accomplishments of doctoral scholars from around the globe.

Our mission continues to be to get research off the coffee table, out of the Ivory Tower of academia, and into the hands of people who cannot only use but benefit from the insights and wisdom found from doctoral research results and findings. Our intention is to continue to bridge the gap from the halls of academia into the halls of the business world. *The Refractive Thinker®* series continues to offer a resource from contributing doctoral scholars as they offer their chapter summaries of doctoral research well beyond the boundaries of a traditional textbook. Instead, the goal for this series is to use refractive thinking strategies to push the boundaries beyond conventional wisdom and to explore the paths not yet traveled, particularly in this evolving digital age.

As we move into the Spring of 2023, this peer-reviewed publication offers readers insights and solutions to various challenges within the realm of criminal justice, whether on the world stage, in the classroom, or in their personal space. Our hope is for you to find answers regarding these unique challenges managers and leaders face in finding effective ethical policies and practices within this field. Within these pages, scholars offer insights regarding emerging trends within criminal justice to include these topics to add their lessons learned from their doctoral level research and their experience regarding how to navigate the Criminal Justice System from the effects of ethical leadership on employee engagement, effective strategies to reduce hospital data breaches, examining the high cost of police misconduct, the effect of criminal justice policies on the business economy, reformed offenders as solutions to the employee shortage, the illusion of education in America's public schools, leaders affecting change for diversity, equity, and inclusion, the courage of thought and why we suspend our thinking, and the mindset shift in higher education, to educate or litigate.

This volume will continue to shape the conversation of future success in business to examine proven effective policies and practices that have come from the research and pens of professional academicians and scholars around the world. The premise is to think not only *outside the box*, but also *beyond the box*, to create new solutions, to ask new questions, to proceed forward on new roads not yet explored or traveled. Our premise is to review academic research in a simple to digest executive summary format to offer new ways for business leaders to think about effective practices for strategies in their business based on what new research has to offer specifically growing the future of business.

With this volume, we continue to include a section to the series where Dr. Cheryl Lentz, *The Academic Entrepreneur*, concludes each chapter from a business point of view to link this doctoral research to applications for your business.

Remember, not only does *The Refractive Thinker*® series offer a physical book, we offer eBooks (Kindle, Nook, and Adobe eReader), and eChapters (individual chapters by author) that highlight the writings of your favorite Refractive Thinker® scholars, available through our website: http://RefractiveThinker.com, as well as Amazon.com. Be sure to visit our social media on

Facebook, Twitter, YouTube, and LinkedIn® for further discussions regarding the ideas presented here.

We look forward to your continued support and interest of the more than 200 scholars within *The Refractive Thinker*® doctoral community who contributed to this multi award winning anthology series from around the globe. Our mission that began with Volume 1 many years ago is to bring research out of academia for application in the world of business to provide answers to the many questions asked.

# Acknowledgments

The foundation of scholarly research embraces the art of asking questions—to validate and affirm what we do, and why. Through asking the right questions, the right answers are found. Leaders often challenge the status quo, to offer alternatives and new directions, to dare to try something bold and audacious, to try something that has never been tried before. This 25th publication of our beloved multiple award-winning *The Refractive Thinker*® series required the continued belief in this new publishing model, of a peer-reviewed doctoral anthology, by those willing to continue forward on this voyage. (This is Vol. XXIII, however, we published Vol. II three times!)

We are grateful for the help of many who made this collaboration possible. First, let me offer a special thank you to our **Peer Review Board**, to include Dr. Judy Blando, Dr. Karen Balcanoff, Dr. Ed Jordan, and myself; and our and media partner, Rebecca Hall-Gruyter and her amazing team.

My gratitude extends with a well-deserved thank you to our production team: Gary Rosenberg (production specialist) and Joey Root, designer of the original Refractive Thinker logo.

Thank you. We appreciate everyone's contributions to this scholarly collaboration.

Job well done!
My best to our continued success!

**Dr. Cheryl Lentz**
Managing Editor and Chief Refractive Thinker

CHAPTER 1

# Sustaining Small Businesses Through Criminal Justice and Employee Retention

## Dr. Anastasia Persad & Dr. JaQuane Jones

Small businesses play a role in the economy of any country. They face challenges to remain sustainable. One factor determining the sustainability of small businesses is the Criminal Justice System and its ever-changing policies. The Criminal Justice System influences small businesses' ability to remain sustainable including employee retention, fair compensation, and safety. Recognizing the indispensable contributions of small businesses to the economy and the potential adverse effects of crime on their long-term viability, the Criminal Justice System establishes collaborative relationships with these entities (Gaines et al., 2021). The practice of supporting sustainability for small businesses requires the Criminal Justice System to create, maintain and enforce rules and regulations that allow for improving the social and environmental impacts (Barbosa et al., 2020).

In this chapter, the goal is to explore how the Criminal Justice System affects small businesses' sustainability and the policies that support their success. We delve into the relationship between small business sustainability and the environment, fair compensation, and employee retention. The analysis demonstrates the importance of these factors in small business sustainability and how they relate to the Criminal Justice System. Studies carried out in the United States showed the importance of small businesses for the economy in the locations where they operate (Barbosa et al., 2020). For all countries, sustainability is an important topic. Small businesses can create profitable and competitive advantages through developing effective sustainability strategies. The implications of our findings apply to policymakers, business owners, and other stakeholders involved in small business sustainability.

## Small Business Sustainability and the Criminal Justice System

The Criminal Justice System plays a role in small business sustainability by influencing factors such as the environment, employee retention, fair compensation, and safety (Persad, 2020). This guiding role fosters a sustainable business environment, reducing crime in local communities, and improving families' standard of living (Jones, 2021; Liu & Li, 2022). Criminal justice continues to influence the efforts to attain sustainable development of small businesses by regulating the limitations of market-based decision making (Hoffman, 2000). Sustainable development is relevant to the general discussion of crime and its influence on crime. Some researchers insist that sustainability of small businesses should be an endless quest because of its influence on criminal justice policies and practices (Kopnina, 2017).

Small business sustainability is important for crime prevention in local communities where the businesses are located. The Criminal Justice System actively supports this factor of small business sustainability by creating and enforcing laws and regulations to prevent environmental degradation (Hoffman, 2000). These policies provide ongoing employment opportunities, job training, fair and equal compensation, and a safe working environment for local community members. The Criminal Justice System influences the sustainability of small businesses by providing lawful alternatives to individuals when they are facing difficult situations (Levenson, 2021). Small businesses that remain sustainable seek to enrich the community by providing much needed services, increasing employment opportunities, and reducing crime rates.

## The Criminal Justice System's Effect on Employee Retention

Employee retention is integral to running a successful business, as it contributes to small business sustainability. The U.S. national average turnover rate was 47.2% (U.S. Bureau of Labor Statistics, 2022). Retaining skilled and knowledgeable employees, whether established or recently hired, is a primary factor in small business sustainability. To reduce unwanted employee turnover, owners and leaders of small businesses should focus on practices that include employee safety-related training, ongoing job training, fair and equal compensation, and promoting a healthy work-life balance. Satisfied employees exhibit fewer turnover intentions; job satisfaction, working in a safe environment, employee retention, and small business sustainability are directly correlated (Chiedu et al., 2017). Reducing expenses and unexpected staffing changes can increase performance effectiveness and generate financial cost savings, leading to increased small business sustainability (Delmar et al., 2013).

A study of 290 employees working for the same restaurant chain in different locations across the United States revealed that unsafe working conditions, lack of training, unequal and unfair compensation, and an unhealthy work-life balance, affected employees' job embeddedness (Tews et al., 2014). These factors triggered intentions of seasoned and newly hired employees to leave their current organization and seek employment elsewhere. It was revealed that other factors such as negative workplace gossip demoralized employees, affected their psychological and physical well-being which resulted in job dissatisfaction (Persad,

2020). Employees are the most important asset of a small business and retaining them is one of the toughest challenges for small businesses as they work towards sustainability. The Criminal Justice System's role in protecting employees has grown significantly due to ever-changing technology, increased competition, and globalization (Singh, 2021).

Fair compensation is important to small business sustainability and the Criminal Justice System is intervening to ensure workers receive fair pay. In the United States, the minimum wage does not equate to a living wage, with costs of living increasing while salaries remain stagnant. The U.S. Small Business Administration (SBA) (2019) reported that small businesses constitute 99.7% of U.S. firms. With pay transparency not federally required, employers can pay employees less than the average compensation for a position (Smit & Montag-Smit, 2019). Pay transparency in the workplace is growing and it is unclear which factors entice employees to share pay information. Individual states take a different approach to pay transparency and their legislative bodies have enacted laws to address pay communication policies. Pay transparency policies can lead to more accurate information about earnings potential which increases employee motivation and productivity (Cullen, 2023). Historically, the Criminal Justice System has protected employers, however states like New York require all employers to publish compensation information including minimum salary for all job postings. Fair pay and a living wage offers benefits to workers, their families, communities, and small business sustainability (Aitken et al., 2019).

Criminal Justice System policies guide small business sustainability, influencing factors such as the working environment, employee retention, equal and fair compensation, and safety (Jones, 2021; Liu & Li, 2022). Criminal Justice System policies support small business sustainability by providing local community members with employment opportunities, job training, fair and equal compensation, a safe environment, and improved standards of living. Fair compensation is important to small business sustainability, and the Criminal Justice System is increasingly intervening to ensure workers receive fair pay. In the United States, the minimum wage does not equate to a living wage, and as the cost-of-living increases, salaries often do not keep up. Without a U.S. federal pay transparency requirement, employers can pay employees less than the average compensation for their positions.

## The Criminal Justice System's Effect on Employee Safety and Environmental Sustainability

Small businesses must prioritize employee safety and environmental sustainability to ensure long-term success. The Criminal Justice System plays a role in establishing and enforcing regulations that safeguard workers and the environment. There has been an increased focus on the intersection of environmental protection, employee safety, and criminal justice (Gray & Silbey, 2014). The Occupational Safety and Health Administration (OSHA) (2021) enforces workplace safety regulations and provides guidelines that small businesses must follow to maintain a safe working environment. Ensuring employee safety diminishes workplace injuries and accidents, contributing to employee satisfaction and retention, both essential to small business sustainability (Jones, 2021).

The Criminal Justice System's role in protecting the environment proves significant for small business sustainability. Environmental crimes, such as illegal dumping, air and water pollution, and other harmful practices, can negatively and adversely affect the communities in which small businesses operate. The U.S. Environmental Protection Agency (EPA) (2021) enforces regulations to prevent and address these issues. Small businesses must adhere to EPA guidelines to ensure their operations remain environmentally sustainable and reduce the risk of legal ramifications. By complying with environmental regulations, small businesses contribute to a healthier community and a sustainable future.

The Criminal Justice System can help small businesses improve their sustainability practices by providing incentives and support. Tax breaks, grants, and low-interest loans are available for small businesses that invest in environmentally friendly practices (SBA, 2021). These incentives promote environmental sustainability and help small businesses stay competitive in the market. Small businesses can take advantage of training and resources provided by the government to enhance their sustainability practices and ensure compliance with environmental regulations.

The Criminal Justice System plays a role in advancing small business sustainability through the assurance of employee safety and environmental protection. By enforcing regulations that keep workers safe and the environment clean, the Criminal Justice System supports a healthier and sustainable future for communities and small businesses. Through incentives and support, the Criminal Justice System encourages small businesses to adopt environmentally friendly practices, contributing to their long-term success. The role of the Criminal Justice System in small business sustainability is significant, emphasizing the importance of compliance with safety and environmental regulations for continued growth and success. Small business owners can identify ways to integrate environmental and social responsibility into their operations, promoting sustainability and contributing to a healthier future for communities.

## Stakeholder Collaboration for Small Business Sustainability Through Criminal Justice

Within the realm of criminal justice and its influence on small business sustainability, several key stakeholders contribute to the process. These stakeholders encompass law enforcement agencies, the judicial system, local and national governments, community organizations, and small business owners (Demir et al., 2020).

Law enforcement agencies, including the police, foster small business sustainability by curbing criminal activity (Perez et al., 2020). Tasked with patrolling communities, responding to emergencies, and investigating crimes, they can collaborate with small businesses and engage communities to identify and address areas of concern (Squires, 2019). They can advise small business proprietors on effective security measures and crime prevention strategies (Bowers, 2001).

The judicial system, comprising prosecutors and judges, enforces criminal laws and penalizes those who violate them (Demir et al., 2020). By holding perpetrators accountable for their actions, the judicial system ensures that small businesses are shielded from criminal activity and cultivate a fair and predictable legal environment conducive to small business stability and investment in local communities.

Local and national governments play a role in enhancing small business sustainability through criminal justice policies (Demir et al., 2020). Policies can allocate funding to law enforcement and community organizations, promote small business development through grants and initiatives, and create laws and regulations that safeguard small businesses from criminal activities while fostering a just and stable legal environment.

Community organizations, including neighborhood watch groups and business associations, are instrumental in advancing small business sustainability via crime prevention and community engagement (Squires, 2019). They can collaborate with law enforcement and small business owners to pinpoint areas of concern and devise strategies to minimize the likelihood of criminal (Taylor et al., 2023). Community organizations can support small businesses affected by crime, providing resources and guidance for recovery (Jones, 2021).

Small business owners are important stakeholders in promoting sustainability through criminal justice (Jones, 2021). By adopting measures to protect their enterprises from criminal activities, forming partnerships with law enforcement, and participating in community organizations, they can actively contribute to enhancing safety and security in their local communities. Small business owners can advocate for policies that create a fair and predictable legal environment for small businesses.

Criminal justice stakeholders as it pertains to small business sustainability include law enforcement agencies, the judicial system, local and national governments, community organizations, and small business owners (Demir et al., 2020). Through their collective efforts, a safe and supportive environment for small businesses can be established, which benefits local communities and the economy.

## Criminal Justice System's Role in Fair Compensation for Small Businesses

In the United States, the current federal minimum wage does not provide a living wage for workers, leaving many struggling to afford essential expenses such as housing, food, and transportation. According to the Department of Health and Human Services (HHS) (2021), the poverty guideline for a single person in the contiguous United States is $13,011 per year. Small businesses, which make up 99.7% of U.S. firms, rely on fair compensation for employee retention and job satisfaction (Persad, 2020). While pay transparency is not federally mandated, Criminal Justice System players, including state attorney generals, district attorneys, and criminal prosecutors, are increasingly prosecuting employers for wage theft, promoting fair compensation and enhancing the sustainability of small businesses.

Workers deserve a living wage and fair pay, which benefits their families and communities, and small business sustainability (Aitken et al., 2019). This practice represents a historic shift in the Criminal Justice System, as crimes against workers are rarely prosecuted. The Criminal Justice System protects employees by mandating that businesses, regardless of their size, disclose starting salaries and compensation packages in job postings in certain states like New York. Employee turnover affects a company's bottom line, regardless of the industry, and small businesses are no different (Persad, 2020). Reducing expenses and unexpected staffing changes in an organization may increase performance effectiveness and generate financial cost savings (Delmar et al., 2013; Jones, 2021), leading to improved sustainability of small businesses.

The Criminal Justice System's role in promoting fair compensation is crucial to small business sustainability. By ensuring a living wage and pay transparency, the Criminal Justice System will ensure an equitable working environment that supports the long-term success of small businesses. This shift toward protecting workers' rights reflects the growing recognition of the importance of fair compensation for the sustainability of small businesses and the well-being of communities (Jones, 2021; Persad, 2020).

## Promoting Fair Compensation for Small Business Sustainability

Small businesses constitute a significant portion of the U.S. economy, accounting for 99.7% of firms in the country (SBA, 2019). Fair compensation and a living wage are important for the sustainability of these businesses, as they contribute to employee retention and job satisfaction (Persad, 2020). The Criminal Justice System ensures that workers receive fair pay by prosecuting wage theft and advocating for policies that require transparency in compensation.

The cost of living in the United States has steadily increased, rendering essentials such as housing, food, and transportation less affordable for workers (Bureau of Labor Statistics, 2021). The minimum wage falls short of providing a living wage, and in the absence of federal requirements for pay transparency, employers may underpay their employees (Persad, 2020). To address this issue, state attorney generals, district attorneys, and criminal prosecutors are pursuing cases against employers engaged in wage theft. This change in focus represents a historic shift in the Criminal Justice System, which previously protected employers rather than workers.

Certain states, including New York, mandate that employers disclose the starting salary and compensation package in their job postings, thus promoting pay transparency and equitable compensation practices. Fair pay and a living wage offers advantages to workers, their communities, and the long-term sustainability of small businesses (Aitken et al., 2019). Employee turnover can effect a company's financial performance, and small businesses are no different (Persad, 2020). By reducing expenses and unexpected staffing changes in the organization, performance effectiveness can be increased, and financial cost savings can be generated, leading to enhanced sustainability for small businesses (Delmar et al., 2013; Jones, 2021).

The Criminal Justice System's role in promoting fair compensation and living wages is significant for the sustainability of small businesses. By prosecuting wage theft and advocating for pay transparency, the Criminal Justice System is working to protect workers' rights and ensure that small businesses can thrive. As the cost of living continues to rise, small businesses and the Criminal Justice System must work together to support fair compensation and promote sustainable business practices.

## Conclusion

The Criminal Justice System supports small business sustainability by enforcing rules and policies that encourage environmental preservation, employee retention, fair compensation, and secure work environments. By making business owners responsible, the Criminal Justice System cultivates an equitable setting where small businesses can compete and grow. The Criminal Justice System's attention to issues like wage theft and pay transparency ensures that workers receive just treatment, which bolsters small business sustainability.

The Criminal Justice System's collaboration with other stakeholders, such as local and national authorities, develops a multifaceted approach to addressing challenges and fostering a supportive environment for small businesses. This joint effort contributes to a resilient economy capable of navigating market shifts and uncertainties. The Criminal Justice System's dedication to environmental and social responsibility can encourage ethical business practices, leading to a sustainable and inclusive economic landscape. As an important part of the U.S. economy, small businesses need ongoing support from the Criminal Justice System and other stakeholders to promote sustainable growth and positively affect their communities.

## THOUGHTS FROM THE ACADEMIC ENTREPRENEUR

*The Problem to be Solved:*

- Establishing a criminal justice framework that fortifies small business endurance by addressing employee retention, equitable compensation, key stakeholders, and occupational safety and well-being.

*The Goals:*

- To explore the relationship between the Criminal Justice System and small business sustainability.
- To advocate for fair compensation and pay transparency in small businesses and highlight the role of the Criminal Justice System in protecting workers from wage theft.
- To raise awareness of the effect of the Criminal Justice System on small businesses and encourage policymakers to consider the needs of small business owners in their decisions.

*The Questions to Ask:*

- How does the Criminal Justice System affect small business sustainability?
- What are the factors that influence small business sustainability?
- What strategies could law enforcement agencies and community organizations employ to effectively collaborate in addressing crime-related challenges confronting small businesses?
- What policies and regulations are implemented to prevent environmental degradation and promote small business sustainability?

*Today's Business Application:*

- Advocating for policy changes: Small businesses can work with local and national governments to advocate for policies that create a fair and predictable legal environment, support crime prevention efforts, and promote small business development.

- Accessing financial support: Small businesses can seek grants and loans from governmental and non-governmental sources to invest in security measures, business expansion, and recovery from the effects of criminal activities.

- Promoting transparency and trust: Small businesses can build trust within their communities by operating with integrity, adhering to regulations, and being transparent in their business practices. This can help to create a positive perception and reinforce the stability of the small business sector.

# REFERENCES

Aitken, A., Dolton, P., & Riley, R. (2019). The impact of the introduction of the national living wage on employment, hours and wages. *National Institute of Economic and Social Research, Discussion Paper, 501.* https://ideas.repec.org/p/nsr/niesrd/501.html

Barbosa, M., Castañeda-Ayarza, J. A., & Ferreira, D. (2020). Sustainable strategic management (GES): Sustainability in small business. *Journal of Cleaner Production, 258,* 120880. https://doi.org/10.1016/j.jclepro.2020.120880

Bowers, K. (2001). Small business crime: The evaluation of a crime prevention initiative. *Crime Prevention and Community Safety, 3*(1), 23-42. https://doi.org/10.1057/palgrave.cpcs.8140079

Bureau of Labor Statistics. (2021). *Consumer price index.* U.S. Department of Labor. https://www.bls.gov/cpi/

Chiedu, K. C., Long, S. C., & Ashar, H. B. (2017). The relationship among job satisfaction, organizational commitment and employees' turnover at Unilever corporation in Nigeria. *European Journal of Multidisciplinary Studies, 5*(1), 370-383. https://doi.org/ 10.26417/ejms.v5i1.p370-383

Cullen, Z. B. (2023). *Is pay transparency good?* (No. w31060). National Bureau of Economic Research. https://doi.org/10.3386/w31060

Delmar, F., McKelvie, A., & Wennberg, K. (2013). Untangling the relationships among growth, profitability and survival in new firms. *Technovation, 33*(8-9), 276-291. https://doi.org/10.1016/j.technovation.2013.02.003

Demir, M., Apel, R., Braga, A. A., Brunson, R. K., & Ariel, B. (2020). Body worn cameras, procedural justice, and police legitimacy: A controlled experimental evaluation of traffic stops. *Justice Quarterly, 37*(1), 53-84. https://doi.org/10.1080/07418825.2018.1495751

Gaines, L. K., Kappeler, V. E., & Powell, Z. A. (2021). *Policing in America* (9th ed.). Routledge. https://doi.org/10.4324/9781315267456

Gray, G., & Silbey, S. (2014). Governing inside the organization: Interpreting regulation and compliance. *American Journal of Sociology, 120*(1), 96-145. https://doi.org/10.1086/676403

Hoffman, J. (2000). Sustainable economic development: A criminal justice challenge for the 21st century. *Crime, Law and Social Change, 34,* 275-299. https://doi.org/10.1023/A:1008360426802

Jones, J. M. (2021). Strategies to overcome constraints for small business sustainability (10344). *Walden Dissertations and Doctoral Studies.* https://scholarworks.waldenu.edu/dissertations/10344

Kopnina, H. (2017). Sustainability: New strategic thinking for business. *Environment, Development and Sustainability, 19,* 27-43. https://doi.org/10.1007/s10668-015-9723-1

Levenson, L. L. (2021). Climate change and the Criminal Justice System. *Environmental Law, 51*(2), 333-381. https://www.jstor.org/stable/27027144

Liu, X., & Li, S. (2022). The impact of criminal law regulation-based business environment optimization on entrepreneurial spirit and enterprise development. *Front Psychology, 13*, 1-15. https://doi.org/10.3389/fpsyg.2022.944146

Occupational Safety and Health Administration (OSHA). (2021). *U.S. Department of Labor.* http://www.osha.gov

Persad, A. (2020). Strategies to retain skilled assistant project managers in construction industries (9621). *Walden Dissertations and Doctoral Studies.* https://scholarworks.waldenu.edu/dissertations/9621

Singh, D. (2019). A literature review on employee retention with focus on recent trends. *International Journal of Scientific Research in Science and Technology, 6*(1), 425-431. https://doi.org/10.32628/IJSRST195463

Smit, B. W., & Montag-Smit, T. (2019). The pay transparency dilemma: Development and validation of the pay information exchange preferences scale. *Journal of Applied Psychology, 104*(4), 537-558. https://doi.org/10.1037/apl0000355

Squires, P. (2019). Community safety and crime prevention. In (Ed.), *Handbook of crime prevention and community safety* (pp. 32–54). Routledge. https://doi.org/10.4324/9781315724393-3

Taylor, R. B., Lockwood, B., & Wyant, B. R. (2023). Can street block 311 physical incivility call count shifts predict later changing on-site conditions?: Gauging ecological construct validity of 311 litter calls. *Journal of Crime and Justice.* https://doi.org/10.1080/0735648X.2022.2157862

Tews, M. J., Stafford, K., & Michel, J. W. (2014). Life happens and people matter: Critical events, constituent attachment, and turnover among part-time hospitality employees. *International Journal of Hospitality Management, 38*, 99-105. https://doi.org/10.1016/j.ijhm.2014.01.005

U.S. Bureau of Labor Statistics. (2022). *Job openings and labor turnover summary.* https://data.bls.gov

U.S. Department of Health and Human Services. (2021). 2021 poverty guidelines computations. Office of the Assistant Secretary for Planning and Evaluation. https://aspe.hhs.gov/topics/poverty-economic-mobility/poverty-guidelines/prior-hhs-poverty-guidelines-federal-register-references/2021-poverty-guidelines/2021-poverty-guidelines-computations

U.S. Environmental Protection Agency (EPA). (2021). *Laws and regulations.* https://www.epa.gov/laws-regulations

U.S. Small Business Administration (SBA). (2019). *SBA Agency Financial Report-FY 2019.* U.S. Small Business Administration's FY 2019 Agency Financial Report (AFR). https://www.sba.gov/sites/default/files/2019-12/SBA_FY_2019_AFR-508.pdf

## *About the Authors...*

**Dr. Anastasia Persad** hails from Berbice, Guyana. She grew up in Queens, New York, and currently resides in South Florida. Dr. Persad, affectionately known as Dr. Ana to her colleagues and mentees, is a Commercial Construction Project Manager at HITT Contracting in their Fort Lauderdale office. She has overseen construction projects up to $80M with a specialization in construction concierge services.

Dr. Ana serves as a board member and the Director of Business Management for the Humanitarian Mission of Guyana. She is also a committee member of the Black Leadership Network ERG, Building Leaders ERG, Women of HITT ERG, and the HITT Pride Alliance.

She is an ordained minister, professional announcer, business coach, life coach, and small business owner. Dr. Ana volunteers at organizations including the Humanitarian Mission of Guyana, Meals on Wheels, and the One Love Foundation. Dr. Ana is an active member of the National Association of Women in Construction and the National Association of Professional Women.

To reach **Dr. Ana Persad** for information on refractive thinking, professional editing, or guest speaking, please **e-mail**: DrAnaPersad@gmail.com

**Dr. JaQuane (Jay) Jones, Sr.,** an esteemed reserve active-duty Medical Military Officer in the United States Army, is acclaimed for his unrivaled expertise in strategic leadership and business management. He holds two distinguished doctoral degrees: a Doctorate in Strategic Leadership from Liberty University and a Doctorate in Business Administration from Walden University. As a valued member of the American College of Healthcare Executives (ACHE), Dr. Jay contributes to the advancement of healthcare management. In addition to his military and healthcare accomplishments, Dr. Jay serves as a college professor at South College, where he imparts his extensive knowledge in finance through an array of courses, including Corporate

Finance, Foundations of Personal Financial Management, Financial Markets & Institutions, Investment Management, and Case Studies in Financial Analysis.

An accomplished scholar, Dr. Jay conducts comprehensive research in business, leadership, healthcare management, and finance. His groundbreaking studies have provided invaluable insights, playing an important role in advancing these respective fields. As an initiate of the Kappa Beta Chapter of Kappa Alpha Psi Fraternity, Inc., and a proud member of the Fort Knox Alumni Chapter, Dr. Jay remains dedicated to fostering camaraderie and collaboration.

With years of experience and research, Dr. Jay has established himself as an eminent authority in his field. Additional published works include his dissertation: *Strategies to Overcome Constraints for Small Business Sustainability, SME Sustaining Strategies*. His unparalleled knowledge and unwavering dedication have made him a highly sought-after resource among colleagues and professionals. As an esteemed and respected figure in academic and professional circles, Dr. Jay embodies the essence of an expert professional scholar.

To reach **Dr. JaQuane (Jay) Jones, Sr.** for additional information or guest speaking, please visit his **website:** http://www.DrJaQuaneJonesLeadership.com or **e-mail:** drJonesJ@gmail.com

CHAPTER 2

# Effective Strategies to Reduce Data Breach in Hospitals

## Dr. Frank Musmar

Fifty million Americans were affected by health records data breaches in 2022 (Mansfield-Devine, 2022). Researchers to date offer little information on the strategies to protect hospitals from data breaches (Barati, 2022). Data breaches negatively affect a patient's life and security (Tang, 2022). Identifying strategies to reduce data breaches may reduce hospital reputational damage and remediation costs and protect patients' security. The federal Act 18 U.S.C 1030 is a mechanism for persecuting cybercrimes, including hacking and data breaching, and provides both criminal and civil penalties ranging from 10 to 20 years of imprisonment.

Hospital leaders use data communication and web-based technology to manage organizational activities (Mansfield-Devine, 2022). Hackers use information-based technology data to access financial and private data (Barati, 2022). Hackers are people or entities illegally accessing unauthorized information. Illegally obtaining information violates data security measures that security officers create, potentially costing hospitals billions of dollars (Tang, 2022). Accordingly, learning the strategies to enhance security, safety, and reduce data breaches is essential.

Tosoni (2020) reported that nearly 984 data security breaches resulted in the theft of 10 million private records. Small and medium enterprises (SMEs) experienced approximately 72%

of the 984 data security breaches (Tosoni, 2020). Hackers target patients' records because they contain detailed information. Hospital owners may experience bankruptcy if they encounter a security breach (Alunge, 2020). Some retailers have lost as much as $291 million on one breach-related activity (Alunge, 2020). Providing small business owners with the strategies needed to reduce data security breaches could reduce data security breaches as well as their liability within the judicial courts and courts of public opinion. The purpose of the Musmar (2023) study was to explore effective strategies to reduce data breaches in hospitals. I interviewed 10 hospital leaders in the United States who worked in the position for at least 2 years.

## Data Security in Hospitals

Hospital leaders should implement data protection plans (Barati & Yankson, 2022) to address corporate liability, privacy, and security. Hospital leaders experience challenges managing the risk of fraudulent activities, including their ability to protect their operations from detecting fraud (Barati & Yankson, 2022). Hospital leaders must implement security measures to prevent negative financial influence on performance. Hospitals receive large amounts of data from their business partners with minimum security (Wairimu & Fritsch, 2022). As a result, hospital leaders who fail to implement a secure information technology (IT) infrastructure may experience cyber-attacks. Some hospital leaders fail to implement adequate cybersecurity plans because they do not believe they could become cyber targets (Alunge, 2020). Because of inadequate cybersecurity plans, hospital leaders are often unprepared to handle data security breaches (Alunge, 2020). In a study involving 400 hospitals, 32% had not implemented enough cybersecurity methods (Alunge, 2020), leaving them vulnerable to legal liability in the courts. Approximately 55% of the participants failed to reinforce their security protocols to prevent possible security breaches costing hospitals billions of dollars (Alunge, 2020).

Approximately 45% of hospital leaders have not implemented a contingency plan to respond to a security breach (Data Breach, 2020). Implementing a contingency plan could reduce the recovery time or the chances of experiencing a cyber-attack (Data Breach, 2020). Hospital leaders should implement a contingency plan to handle sudden blackouts and natural disasters (Data Breach, 2020). In 2020, the U.S. Secret Service reviewed approximately 960 data breaches; 45% of the breaches occurred at hospitals (Burton, 2020). Cybercriminals target hospitals because they have detailed patient information (Burton, 2020). Data breaches in hospitals compromise consumers' private information and companies are vulnerable to professional liability in the courts.

The hospitals' main point of sale has been through insurance and credit card payments, with as much as 66% of all transactions made through credit card payments (Cao et al., 2023). Dishonest employees' access to data threatens data security (Cao et al., 2023). Hospitals must have automatic antivirus software, regular self-assessment, a security plan, and periodic network evaluation (Cao et al., 2023). From the hacker's perspective, the interconnected relationship between insurance companies and hospitals underscores the importance of protecting the point of sale and data transformation (Ighravwe & Mashao, 2019). Hackers can steal data such as names, social security numbers, email addresses, phone numbers, and addresses (Ighravwe & Mashao, 2019). This information allows hackers to gain access to protected websites (Ighravwe & Mashao, 2019).

Tang (2022) suggested that hospital IT specialists secure their wireless systems, telecommuting communications, and electronic emails. The National Institute of Standards and Technology

(NIST) developed an eScan Security Assessment tool as a security strategy to inform hospitals about their IT systems (Tang, 2022). IT personnel can use the system to identify the level of protection against cyber-attacks and use the eScan Security Assessment tool to obtain a series of security questions to test the level of protection in their hospitals, such as contingency plans, security policies, and system failure policies (Tang, 2022). IT specialists can use the NIST report results for suggestions on data security improvement.

Investing in cybersecurity could improve organizational performance. Hospital leaders should invest in cybersecurity to prevent the cost of a future cyber incident (Adharsh & Vijayalakshmi, 2022). Delaying the implementation of security methods could increase the chance of hospital leaders experiencing a security breach (Adharsh & Vijayalakshmi, 2022). When hospital leaders do not adopt a reliable security measure, infrastructure, or policy, several legal and financial implications will affect their organization (Adharsh & Vijayalakshmi, 2022). For instance, neglecting to implement data security practices properly could result in receiving a fine from the Federal Trade Commission (FTC) (Adharsh & Vijayalakshmi, 2022). The FTC intervened on behalf of the customers and filed cases against companies for not adequately protecting consumers' data (Adharsh & Vijayalakshmi, 2022). Each settlement ordered by the FTC could result in 20 years of costly and time-consuming remedial data security processes.

## Implementing Policies and Procedures to Prevent Data Breaches

Securing data is a challenging and continuous process for hospital leaders (Thomas et al., 2022). Failure to comply with or implement information security policies and procedures may cause hospital leaders to experience a security breach (Thomas et al., 2022). The development and implementation of formal policies are necessary to protect organizational data (Thomas et al., 2022). These policies and procedures must evolve to address the rapid changes in data security threats. Data breaches occur because a user fails to comply with information security policies (Greenwood & Vaaler, 2022). Employees pose the greatest threat to organizations (Greenwood & Vaaler, 2022). Employees not adhering to information security guidelines may place the organization at risk (Greenwood & Vaaler, 2022). Employee awareness and education contribute to effective data security strategies. Therefore, hospital leaders must focus on employee training to mitigate vulnerabilities and potential litigation.

Employee behavior toward policies and procedures may affect reliable data protection (Brennan, 2022). Employees' intent to comply with internet policies influenced internet abuse and the costs of noncompliance, with proper sanction risks and possible internet security risks. Brennan (2022) conducted a study regarding the influence of habitual employee behavior and information systems security. Brennan used protection motivation as a theoretical lens and found that employees' habits influenced their decision to comply with information security policies. Employees' habits influenced employees' decisions to comply with security policies based on the threat level. Brennan also discovered that system vulnerability did not affect an employee's decision to comply with information system policies.

Hospital leaders should implement security policies and procedures for access control (Greenwood & Vaaler, 2022). Organizational leaders use control frameworks to establish internal controls to decrease risk. Access control policies are auditable and used to control authorized network access (Greenwood & Vaaler, 2022). Dionysiou and Athanasopoulos (2022) studied government employees' behaviors toward complying with information security policies and procedures. They found that an employee's management rank could influence the outcomes of resources and the results of others in the organization. While researchers advised using security policies as a valid data protection technique, many organizations have yet to adopt the idea that an employee's management position could influence their decision to comply with the rules.

Business leaders use security policies to identify the roles and responsibilities of the employees to protect the systems in their organization (Ighravwe & Mashao, 2019). Hospital leaders implement security policies and procedures to address electronic communication standards, data protection, code of conduct, and physical security (Ighravwe & Mashao, 2019). Employees and users should require signing an electronic agreement to access web-based and digital tools (Tosoni, 2020). Hospital leaders should implement a training mechanism to educate users on the possibility of risking private information (Tosoni, 2020). Implementing and using policies and procedures may help hospital leaders avoid a security breach. Hospital leaders should continue to find ways to implement the appropriate policies and procedures to protect the business and consumers (Tosoni, 2020).

## Strategies to Protect Organizational Data

The most common data security strategies that reduce hospital data breaches, reputational damage, and remediation costs and protect patients' security include password platforms, employee education, data backups, IT, and organizational alignment.

## The Password Platforms Strategy

While many sophisticated techniques protect data from unwanted intruders, password protection remains standard (Tang, 2022).

Passwords are a means to prevent hackers from stealing an individual's or an organization's private information (Tang, 2022). Weak passwords are common approaches by users because they struggle to remember strong passwords (Torrie et al., 2022). Hackers can hack systems where users choose weak passwords (Torrie et al., 2022). While users are educated and aware of good password practices, they still choose to make poor password decisions. Sharing passwords across multiple platforms is common among older and young generations (Torrie et al., 2022). Users create vulnerabilities by reusing the same password to access different applications. Another poor security behavior is storing passwords in vaults to prevent users from forgetting passwords; however, these password vaults are prime targets for hackers (Güven et al., 2022).

The use of graphical passwords is becoming popular to mitigate security vulnerabilities. Applying graphical passwords on small devices requires quality equipment to display images and maintain proper data storage (Güven et al., 2022). Graphical passwords may overcome the drawbacks discovered when using passwords and pin-based authentication (Güven et al., 2022). Other non-alphanumeric password schemes include multifactor authentication, passwords, fingerprints, and iris scans (Güven et al., 2022).

With the proliferation of technology, users' methods of communication have evolved (Kesari, 2022). Developers have created authentication methods such as a three-party password-based authentication key (Kesari, 2022). The authentication key allows users to create a shared cryptographic key from a trusted server to create a standard key among the users sharing the server (Kesari, 2022). The key blocks hackers from intercepting communication using a dictionary attack (Kesari, 2022). This process lets users communicate securely over a public network (Kesari, 2022). Accordingly, passwords are standard security measures used to protect data from intrusion from hackers (Greenwood & Vaaler, 2022). If effectively used, passwords can prevent hackers from stealing an organization's private information.

## Employee Education Strategy

Hospital leaders can reduce data security breaches by adequately training employees (Mould et al., 2022). Creating interactive training with real-life scenarios is beneficial to prevent cyber-attacks (Mould et al., 2022). IT leaders should set employee security training according to employee privileges. Employees responsible for protecting the IT infrastructure should be required to take additional training (Mould et al., 2022). Training the IT specialists to improve the software code's security can improve an organization's data security (Barati & Yankson, 2022). Failure to use secure coding practices could allow malicious intruders to communicate with applications.

## Data Backups Strategy

Data backups are digital libraries that house sensitive information (Feng, 2022). If hospital leaders perform data backups, information is retrievable in case of data loss or breach (Feng, 2022). Data backups allow hospital leaders to prevent service disruption, facilitating data restoration after malicious or unintentional software or hardware failure (de Guise, 2020). Implementing a data backup process could save hospital leaders from data disasters and save time with data restoring efforts because data backups are critical to restoring data in an organization (de Guise, 2020). The security level of the data backups should be equal to the original security level of the primary data source (Li & Chen, 2022). IT leaders should accompany backup plans with a business effect analysis to evaluate the possibility of lost data (Li & Chen, 2022).

## Information Technology and Organizational Alignment

Some hospital leaders are challenged with technology alignment because they lack knowledge and resources (Fast & Overbeck, 2022). Functional alignment positively affects organizational performance when IT competencies complement business and IT capabilities (Fast & Overbeck, 2022). Structural alignment positively affected organizational performance based on IT governance (Fast & Overbeck, 2022).

Tamri and Erwandi (2022) studied academic and operational alignment in organizations. They found that academic alignment did not significantly affect financial performance between I.T and business alignment in the technology transformation and potential competitive alignment. IT alignment did not directly affect financial performance through operational alignment. Academic alignment is apparent when managers align IT and business strategies, whereas operational alignment occurs when leaders align IT, business processes, and infrastructure (Tamri & Erwandi, 2022).

## Effective Strategies to Reduce Data Breach of Hospitals

Hospital leaders can use effective strategies to reduce hospital data breaches, reduce reputational damage and remediation costs, and protect patients' security. In the analysis, P stands for a participant in the findings below, and the number following the P represents the order of interviewed participants. The first participant is P1. The interview data analysis indicated that refractive thinkers who think out of the box and hospital leaders who can implement effective strategies could help their organizations reduce reputational damage and remediation costs by applying information assurance strategy, passwords, secure socket layers (SSL), contingency planning, and relying on third-party data experts. To understand current leadership strategies that hospital leadership uses to reduce hospital data breaches, I interviewed 10 hospital leaders in the United States who worked in their positions for a minimum of 2 years. Below is a discussion of the strategies participants found helpful in reducing hospital data breaches.

## Applying Information Assurance Strategy Reduced Data Breach

This theme emerged from all participants responding to the research questions. All participants used similar phrases when responding to the interview questions. Information assurance is a set of security strategies that protect the data's confidentiality, authentication, integrity, availability, and restoration (Headrick, 2022). Using multiple methods may decrease a company's chances of experiencing a data security breach (Headrick, 2022). The participants provided their existing strategies used to protect their data which varied and consisted of password protection, encryption, and data recovery.

### Passwords

Passwords are still relevant to secure a system, and weak passwords leave the system vulnerable (Curts & Campbell, 2022). The user's inability to remember passwords may cause them to create weak passwords (Curts & Campbell, 2022). P1, P4, and P5 developed websites that required users to create a user ID and password to obtain access to the system. P1, P4, P5, and P7 required employees to use a username and password to access the organization's system. I asked P7 if the business computer was password protected and they stated that the computer was password protected and only P7 had access.

The requirements implemented by P1, P4, P5, and P7 align with the current literature (Curts & Campbell, 2022). Security experts suggested that passwords are a secure method to prevent unwanted access (Curts & Campbell, 2022). Only P9 required employees to change passwords frequently, every 3 to 6 months. Security experts recommend that business leaders implement policies and procedures requiring users to change their passwords every 90 days or less (Headrick, 2022). P10 mentioned a form of two-factor authentication as an additional method to protect data. P10 stated that the employees used a security token in addition to their passwords to access information. The security token was a second method used to identify a user in the system, also known as two-factor authentication. Two-factor authentication strengthens password protection (Headrick, 2022).

## Secure Socket Layer

SSLs contain encryption methods that decrypt messages sent over the network and authenticate the user conducting the action (Simsek et al., 2022). User information, such as credit card and login information, is confidential and protected from hackers when transmitted using SSL encryption (Simsek et al., 2022). P6 stated, "The IT department backs up our data using 256 encryptions of two franchises and two non-franchises. This encryption is part of the highest standards of encryption." Setting an SSL certificate to provide HTTPS protection is a fundamental step for securing your website (Simsek et al., 2022). P5's privacy policy states that " . . . financial transactions are confidential. According to the information in the privacy policy of the corporate office, the system was encrypted using the most recent release of SSL technology with encryption keys of up to 128 bits."

## Contingency Planning

Refractive thinkers apply a contingency response plan to mitigate the loss of services and to continue operations in the case of a security breach or natural disaster (Simsek et al., 2022). Contingency planning allows hospital leaders to respond quickly if they experience a disruption in operation (Teguh Paripurno, 2022). I asked the participants what they would do if a breach occurred. P1 and P8 stated they have a contingency plan if the organization experiences a threat. P2 stated, "If we experience a security breach, all of our data is backed up by the corporate office." P10 mentioned that his IT team uses security measures and a contingency plan, including encryption, firewalls, user ID, and passwords to protect consumers' data. Applying strategies to protect the data is a series of procedures that work together to produce a positive or negative outcome. Knowing the inputs, outputs, and environment increases the performance of the business (Teguh Paripurno, 2022).

## Relying on Third-Party Data Experts Reduced Data Breach

This theme emerged from all participants responding to the research questions. The participants used similar phrases when responding to the interview questions. P5, P7, P9, and P10 indicated that third-party dependency is a crucial factor in enhancing the ability to reduce data security breaches. Third-party dependency emerged from the hospitals' documentation and participants' interview responses. In addition to their IT team, most hospitals relied on third-party companies to back up sensitive data and measure security performance. Third-party data security services can be used to secure data, access content, and store data (Alunge, 2020).

P7 and P8 relied on the corporate offices and IT team for their data security services. P1 and P3 used third-party companies to back up their data. Business owners use data backups to stabilize the organization after experiencing a security breach (Alunge, 2020). P4 stated, "The corporation backs up our data using 256 encryptions. This encryption is part of the highest standards of encryption." P5 stated, "Information is backed up on a server by the corporate office. Our data is backed up hourly on a server." P1 stated, "We are not allowed to backup data on external devices or save any information on our computer drives."

P6 and P8 also used third-party companies to back up their sensitive data. P8 stated, "Sensitive data is backed up through another company. Even if our local computer crashes, we can retrieve our information from the third-party company." P6 stated, "We backup our data with another company." P4, P7, and P10 used third-party companies to monitor performance. Business owners use performance monitoring offered by third-party companies to detect and reduce security breaches (Teguh Paripurno, 2022). P4 and P7 used their corporate offices to monitor their data security performance. P10 stated, "As an individual franchise, we do not measure performance here, but this information is tracked at the corporate level." P4 also stated, "Data security performance is not measured at the organization. Data security performance is measured at our corporate office."

Third-party companies can provide business owners with instant data monitoring. The business owners are alerted if they experience a breach (Teguh Paripurno, 2022). Third-party security monitoring is recommended over business owners installing security applications to monitor performance (de Guise, 2020). The alerts are provided to the business owners to decide what is needed if they experience a breach (Teguh Paripurno, 2022). Measuring performance improves services for business owners with early detection and alerts (Simsek et al., 2022).

## Conclusion

The federal Act 18 U.S.C 1030 is a mechanism for persecuting cybercrimes, including hacking and data breaching, and provides criminal and civil penalties ranging from 10 to 20 years of imprisonment. Hospital leaders can implement effective strategies to reduce data breaches by applying information assurance strategies, passwords, SSLs, contingency planning, and relying on third-party data experts to minimize reputational damage and remediation costs. The participants' techniques help hospital leaders achieve data security, increase productivity, and improve the organization's personal and financial records. Hospital leaders need to consider and implement these strategies to ensure data safety. Implementing these strategies is less expensive than the costs associated with remediation costs. Using this study's findings and recommendations, hospital leaders, scholars, and business leaders will gain new insight into successful strategies shared by experienced professionals. Hospital leaders who can use a refractive thinking approach to implement effective hospital strategies to reduce data breaches might bring long-term success to their organizations.

## THOUGHTS FROM THE ACADEMIC ENTREPRENEUR

*The Problem to be Solved:*
- Improving data security in the healthcare industry
- Reducing data breaches by applying required strategies

*The Goals:*
- Exploring the effective strategies for data security
- Improving organizational performance

*The Questions to Ask:*
- What strategies do hospital leaders use to reduce data security breaches?
- How would your hospital address data security breaches?
- How does your hospital back up sensitive data?
- How are you training your employees to protect your hospital's data from a data security breach?

*Today's Business Application:*
- Hospital leaders with security management skills can reduce data breaches and ensure business sustainability, leading to patient data safety.
- The future of patients' data security depends on hospital leaders understanding data protection strategies.
- Visionary leaders keep effective data breach measures in place.

# REFERENCES

Adharsh, C., & Vijayalakshmi, S. (2022). Prevention of data breach by machine learning techniques. 2022 2nd International Conference on Advance Computing and Innovative Technologies in Engineering *(ICACITE)*. https://doi.org/10.1109/icacite53722.2022.9823523

Alunge, R. (2020). Breach of security vs. personal data breach: Effect on E.U. data subject notification requirements. *International Data Privacy Law, 11*(2), 163-181. https://doi.org/10.1093/idpl/ipaa021

Barati, M. (2022). *Predicting the occurrence of a data breach*. Research Square. https://doi.org/10.21203/rs.3.rs-1594919/v1

Barati, M., & Yankson, B. (2022). Predicting the occurrence of a data breach. *International Journal of Information Management Data Insights, 2*(2). https://doi.org/10.1016/j.jjimei.2022.100128

Brennan, C. (2022). 3. Breach of duty. *Tort Law Directions*, 60-81. https://doi.org/10.1093/he/9780192855367.003.0003

Burton, C. (2020). Article 34 *communication of a personal data breach to the data subject*. The E.U. General Data Protection Regulation (GDPR). https://doi.org/10.1093/oso/9780198826491.003.0070

Cao, H., Phan, H. V., & Silveri, S. (2023). Data breach disclosures and stock price crash risk: Evidence from data breach notification laws. *SSRN Electronic Journal*. https://doi.org/10.2139/ssrn.4393481

Curts, R. J., & Campbell, D. E. (2022). Introduction to information assurance. *Building a global information assurance program*. https://www.oreilly.com/library/view/building-a-global/9780203997550/

Data Breach. (2020). *A user's guide to data protection*: Law and Policy. https://doi.org/10.5040/9781526515735.ch-027

de Guise, P. (2020*). Backup and recovery*. Data Protection, 137-180. https://doi.org/10.1201/9780367463496-12

Dionysiou, A., & Athanasopoulos, E. (2022). Lethe: Practical data breach detection with zero persistent secret state. 2022 IEEE 7th *European Symposium on Security and Privacy* (EuroS&P). https://doi.org/10.1109/eurosp53844.2022.00022

Fast, N. J., & Overbeck, J. R. (2022). The social alignment theory of power: Predicting associative and dissociative behavior in hierarchies. *Research in Organizational Behavior, 42*. https://doi.org/10.1016/j.riob.2022.100178

Feng, D. (2022). Deduplication: *Beginning from data backup system*. Data deduplication for high performance storage system, 1-8. https://doi.org/10.1007/978-981-19-0112-6_1

Greenwood, B., & Vaaler, P. M. (2022). Do U.S. state breach notification laws reduce firm data breaches? *Academy of Management Proceedings, 2022*(1). https://doi.org/10.5465/ambpp.2022.11493abstract

Güven, E. Y., Boyaci, A., & Aydin, M. A. (2022). A novel password policy focusing on altering user password selection habits: A statistical analysis on breached data. *Computers & Security, 113*, 102560. https://doi.org/10.1016/j.cose.2021.102560

Headrick, W. J. (2022). Information assurance in modern A.T.E. 2022. IEEE Autotestcon. https://doi.org/10.1109/autotestcon47462.2022.9984804

Ighravwe, D. E., & Mashao, D. (2019). Development of a differential evolution-based fuzzy cognitive maps for data breach in healthcare sector fuzzy cognitive maps for data breach. 2019 IEEE Africon. https://doi.org/10.1109/africon46755.2019.9134010

Kesari, A. (2022). Do data breach notification laws work? *SSRN Electronic Journal*. https://doi.org/10.2139/ssrn.4164674

Li, X., & Chen, J. (2022). Innovative architecture of college sports online training data based on cloud backup of remote data center. 2022 4th *International Conference on Inventive Research in Computing Applications (ICIRCA)*. https://doi.org/10.1109/icirca54612.2022.9985606

Mansfield-Devine, S. (2022). I.B.M.: Cost of a data breach. *Network Security, 2022*(8). https://doi.org/10.12968/s1353-4858(22)70049-9

Mould, L., Breach, J., & Ledbetter, O. (2022). Evaluation of a training programme to enable M.S.K. physiotherapists to assess ongoing respiratory symptoms in patients with Long COVID. *Physiotherapy, 114*, e136. https://doi.org/10.1016/j.physio.2021.12.095

Simsek, M. M., Ergun, T., & Temucin, H. (2022). SSL test suite: SSL certificate test public key infrastructure. 2022 30th *Signal Processing and Communications Applications Conference (SIU)*. https://doi.org/10.1109/siu55565.2022.9864693

Tamri, T., & Erwandi, R. (2022). Studi tentang kepemimpinan spiritual dan organizational citizenship behavior : Peran otonomi sebagai intervening. *Journal of Administration and Educational Management (ALIGNMENT), 5*(2), 160-176. https://doi.org/10.31539/alignment.v5i2.4443

Tang, A. (2022). Data breach handling. *Privacy in Practice*, 401-413. https://doi.org/10.1201/9781003225089-34

Teguh Paripurno, E. (2022). Participatory contingency plan to C**** 19 adaptation of Merapi volcano eruption - Indonesia. *Progress in Volcanology*. https://doi.org/10.5772/intechopen.98360

Thomas, L., Gondal, I., Oseni, T., & Firmin, S. (2022). A framework for data privacy and security accountability in data breach communications. *Computers & Security, 116*, 102657. https://doi.org/10.1016/j.cose.2022.102657

Torrie, S., Sumsion, A., Sun, Z., & Lee, D.-J. (2022). Facial password data augmentation. *2022 Intermountain Engineering, Technology and Computing (IETC)*. https://doi.org/10.1109/ietc54973.2022.9796673

Tosoni, L. (2020). Article 4(12). *Personal data breach*. The E.U. General Data Protection Regulation (GDPR). https://doi.org/10.1093/oso/9780198826491.003.0018

Wairimu, S., & Fritsch, L. (2022). Modelling privacy harms of compromised personal medical data - beyond data breach. Proceedings of the 17th International Conference on Availability, Reliability, and Security. https://doi.org/10.1145/3538969.3544462

## About the Author . . .

**Dr. Frank Musmar** earned his Doctorate of Business Administration (DBA) in Healthcare Management in 2016 and a Master of Science (MS) in Biotechnology Management in 2011. Dr. Frank is the founder and the Lead Dissertation Consultant at *Editors Dissertations and Thesis*. He has published nine journal publications: *Effective risk management strategies for retail businesses sustainability, The Effect of the Organizational Vision on Remote Employees Engagement, Factors Affecting Millennials Healthcare Employees Turnover, Job Embeddedness and Employee Retention in Healthcare, A Once-daily Oral Medication for Treatment of Cognitive Dysfunction in Down syndrome, Successful Project Management Strategies at Health Care Organizations, Creative Strategies to Enhance Social Media Marketing, Financial Distress at Nonprofit Organizations,* and *Financial Distress in the Health Care Business.*

To reach **Dr. Frank Musmar** for additional information or guest speaking, please visit his website: http://www.editorsdissertationsandthesis.com or **email:** frankmusmar@gmail.com

CHAPTER 3

# The Effect of Ethical Leadership on Employee Engagement: A Moral Approach to Management

## Dr. Kevin Grant

Wherever rules and norms of human coordination and organization are present, people exist who violate these rules and norms, and others are inclined to respond to such violations (Wenzel & Okimoto, 2016). Every country has a system used to manage unlawful acts committed by the public. Criminal justice is a complex system, administered at all levels of government and shaped by a range of actors (Obama, 2017). The topic of this chapter relates to the effect of ethical leadership on employee engagement. The focus of this study was to understand the effective strategies leaders implement to motivate employees in the Criminal Justice System. The policies and practices implemented by government leaders guide the Criminal Justice System. Employees are guided by a leader who is ethical. Ethics is one component of good governance (Perry et al., 2014). The high status, power, and competence of supervisors increase the likelihood that employees will choose them as role models. The supervisors' behaviors signal to employees' expectations and intended norms of the organization.

Being an effective "moral manager" entails keeping problems from escalating to a point that formal regulation might occur (Downe et al., 2016). Hartog (2015) posited that morality is an important topic in organizational behavior and psychology; the attention of researchers for moral and ethical issues in leadership has increased. Researchers found that ethical leadership is important, especially when dealing with cases that can compromise the livelihood of an individual. Halbusi et al. (2020) stated that it is important that managers are motivated to practice ethical leadership because they directly influence the employees. It has been suggested that top managers, especially chief executive officers (CEOs), can shape the ethical climate, which also influences the ethical behavior of employees. Transformational leaders are motivated and practice ethical leadership.

Transformational leaders identify situations that require them to make ethical decisions. Some decisions can have a detrimental outcome. Not all managers display ethical behavior. Despite the importance of supervision quality from the perspective of the correctional officer, quality leadership is not necessarily an innate attribute of all prison wardens (Atkin-Plunk & Armstrong, 2013). Cockcroft (2014) stated that the challenge of understanding the relationship between transactional and transformational leadership and the police means understanding conceptual difficulties associated with leadership models and acknowledging the problems of transposing private sector management models to the public sector. Some leaders abuse their authority and make biased or uninformed decisions. Unethical leadership is destructive leadership. History has shown destructive leadership to be real. Too many countries have been ruled by power-hungry, narcissistic leaders for life, whose destructive ways negatively affect their followers (Kets de Vries et al., 2016).

Through interviews with leaders employed in the Criminal Justice System, I determined which ethical practices are an important aspect of leadership. Leaders who act ethically are respected by their employees. Ethical leaders reflect their respective company so their moral standards affect the organization.

Ethical leaders think in a refractive thinking manner and provide innovative ways of creating ethical environments in an organization. The crucial power of ethical leaders is their ability to actively encourage normatively appropriate behaviors and ensure the ethical and fair treatment of others (Lei et al., 2019).

## Conceptual Framework

Ethical leadership formed the basis of the conceptual framework for this study. The concept of ethical leadership emerged as a prominent theme in the empirical leadership literature, with a dramatic increase in related research since the mid-2000s (Ko et al., 2017). Ko et al. (2017) posited that the concept of ethical leadership is distinct from other prominent types of leadership such as transformational leadership, transactional leadership, spiritual leadership, and authentic leadership. While transformational leaders display ethical leadership, the concept of transformational leadership has various elements not specific to ethical leadership.

Ethics is an important aspect of leadership. In the Criminal Justice System, ethics are important. Leaders are obligated to act in an ethical manner while making decisions that can affect an individual's livelihood. Morality is an important topic in organizational behavior and psychology, and researchers' focus on moral and ethical issues in leadership has increased (Hartog, 2015). Individuals who take on the role of leader in any organization must understand the importance of employee engagement and their obligation to ensure decisions are made based on moral standards.

Leaders who display behavioral ethics make decisions based on society's norms and what is practical in the context of the situation. Ethical leaders are motivational figures in organizations. After establishing when followers moralize their leaders' actions, leaders need to question how moralization influences followers' motivations and behavior. Moralization produces two distinct motivations: (a) a motivation to maintain moral self-regard, and (b) a motivation to maintain a moral reputation (Fehr et al., 2015). Transformational leadership encompasses ethical leadership. Transformational leaders display ethical behavior and make ethical decisions while implementing effective strategies that garner success in the company. Bedi et al. (2015) stated that ethical leaders and idealized influence leaders serve as role models who demonstrate and communicate their ethical values and behaviors to their followers. Ethical leadership overlaps with the individualized consideration dimension of transformational leadership. When employees are treated fairly and respectfully by their leaders, they will think about their relationship with their leader regarding social exchange rather than economic exchange (Engelbrecht et al., 2017).

## Literature Review

Organizations have policies and procedures. These policies are created and implemented by leaders. Leaders must manage ethical issues that occur in the business. Some ethical issues are complex and require consistency in a leader's ethical behavior. In the Criminal Justice System, leaders are faced with making ethical decisions. Leaders must pay close attention to the situation and apply refractive thinking while deciding how to manage the state of affairs in an ethical manner.

Leaders display ethical behavior and implement strategies to motivate employees in their organizations. Displaying ethical behavior shows employees that managers are rational thinkers who understand the consequences of making unethical decisions. Theoretical foundation of ethical leadership suggested that ethical leaders are characterized as honest, caring, and principled individuals who make fair and balanced decisions (Ozbag, 2016). They frequently communicate with their followers about ethics, set clear ethical standards, and use rewards and punishments to see that those standards are followed (Ozbag, 2016). These principles and characteristics are important for leaders in any type of organization. Ethical leaders endorse a broad stakeholder-centric view of the organization; they hold importance, specifically in the current context of the social enterprise as they would ensure that practices undertaken attend to the enterprise's primary objective of stakeholder value maximization (Pasricha et al., 2017). Ethical decisions have a positive effect on employees. The value of the company and how the company is viewed by its customers is improved because of the ethical decisions made by leaders. Customers will have faith in the company and will be comfortable doing business with the organization because of its continued ethical practices. The quality of a company's ethical standards influences consumer perceptions of the company's level of commitment to corporate social responsibility (CSR) (Park et al., 2017). There are benefits to ethical leadership including increasing the credibility of an organization. This will increase the success of the company.

Ashfaq et al. (2021) stated that the growing attention ethical leadership attracts is attributed to its capacity to influence employees' positive attitudes toward everyday assignments at the workplace. The extent of influence that leadership creates on the attitudes and behaviors of employees is not limited to the managerial aspect; nevertheless, it also has ethical implications. Employees respect and are motivated by a leader who makes ethical decisions. Organizations have low employee retention because of leaders who do not display ethical behavior. Most notably, ethical leadership research asserts that the character of an individual leader (exemplified through traits such as honesty and concern for others) is important for fostering positive outcomes in organizations, particularly outcomes associated with their employees such as trust and job satisfaction (Avey et al., 2012). Employees satisfied with their job want to ensure the success of the company. They work in unison with their team and provide constructive feedback on strategies that lead to the achievement of organizational goals.

## Ethical Leadership

Ethical leaders are moral and display moral traits and behaviors in their personal lives. In addition to these personal characteristics, ethical leaders practice moral management, actively influencing employees to be conscientious of ethics and encouraging them to act morally (Ko et al., 2017). Leadership is the demonstration of normatively appropriate conduct through personal actions and interpersonal relationships, and the promotion of such conduct to followers through two-way communication, reinforcement, and decision-making (Brown et al., 2005). An ethical leader's concern for the best interests of their followers, openness to input, fair decision-making, and actively managing morality should result in the leader's attractiveness as a role model (Engelbrecht et al., 2017). Lawton and Pa-ez (2015) suggested that ethical leadership involves some aspects of personal conduct, deemed ethically appropriate, in decision-making and developing relations with others they are inspired to follow.

Ethical behavior should be displayed in all aspects of business. Bavik et al. (2017) posited that ethical leadership has two pillars: a leader must be a moral person (demonstrating moral characteristics and traits in their behavior as a role model) and a moral manager (actively promoting moral principles through two-way and open communication, rewards, and punishment). A leader who inspires others while making moral decisions displays characteristics of a transformational leader. Ethical leaders develop sincere and compassionate relationships with followers who perceive them as supportive in promoting their creativity (Javed et al., 2016). Transformational leaders focus on ethics in an ancillary manner where ethics is one aspect of leadership style (Bedi et al., 2015). Without ethical leadership, the tenets of business ethics will not come to fruition (Bachmann, 2017). A leader is responsible for displaying ethical behavior in the business.

## Applications to Professional Practice

The specific business problem for this study was some business leaders did not use effective ethical strategies to motivate employees in their organizations. Some leaders are seldom faced with a scenario where they must make decisions based on their moral and ethical values. Some leaders do not display the courage or temperance necessary to make ethical decisions in the organization Alam et al. (2021) posited that courage is the ability of an ethical leader to face resistance while acting ethically. Temperance implies exercising restraint from indulging in selfish and covetous excesses. Justice is being fair. Ethical leaders must be fair when making decisions. Ethical leaders must be understanding of every situation and be open minded while maintaining moral standards within an organization.

Ethical leadership has a positive effect on the organization and its employees The findings from the interviews conducted with leaders employed in the Criminal Justice System revealed that ethical leaders who have implemented successful strategies to create a moral environment, motivate employees to achieve organizational goals. Ethical practices are advantageous to leaders and employees and will benefit an organization by improving the moral standard of all staff members Ethical leadership has a significant influence on the way employees interpret decisions with moral import. When leaders practice ethical leadership, employees are not inclined to display deviant conduct (Lazim et al., 2020). The findings from this study include suggestions for leaders to improve ethical practices through refractive thinking in the organization and include improved employee engagement strategies and improved leader and employee communication. Other suggestions included seminars and workshops about ethical business practices for leaders and employees. Employee engagement will improve employee morale and will garner success for the company because the employees operate efficiently when performing their duties.

## Implications for Social Change

The findings of this study add to social change by offering business leaders the opportunity to develop their employees' moral and ethical values by implementing ethical leadership strategies in organizations. Creating an ethical environment in an organization fosters positive thinking and a socially trusting atmosphere. Employees who work in a moral environment will act ethically outside of the organization. Employees develop characteristics that define them as being refractive thinkers who can differentiate between right and wrong. Refractive thinking is equally important in a society where moral standards have deteriorated. Ethical leadership and behavioral approach can be adopted to solve the crisis among employees depending on the situation (Lazim et al., 2020). How a crisis is managed has material and ethical consequences (Branick, 2020). Ethical leadership can also solve crises within society.

Similar to tertiary and secondary academic facilities, businesses assist in the development of an individual's perception on ethical concepts. In organizations where employees are motivated by their leaders, they mimic their leader's behaviors. Leaders who implement ethical strategies in organizations minimize cases of fraud and misappropriation of funds. Creating an ethical culture in an organization has social benefits. Minimal internal scams will occur when ethics is solidly implanted in corporate culture and exemplified by top leadership. Culture is an important mechanism that shapes the behavior of employees and the organization's ethical atmosphere (Ocansey & Ganu, 2017). Employees use ethical behavior in their daily life. Ethical behavior becomes part of their lifestyle and part of their subconscious. These ethical behaviors are seen in households and social environments and can have a positive effect on society. Ethical behavior has a positive effect on society, and effect affects customer relations. Ferrell et al. (2019) suggested that customers maintain personally held expectations toward companies and business ethics practices. Preconceived attitudes of how companies should act have the potential to influence the customer's perception of a company's actual behavior.

## Recommendations for Action

Business leaders need to ascertain if the strategies documented in the findings of this study are appropriate to their type of business. Ethical leaders know the importance of employee engagement and encourage their employees through effective engagement strategies that stimulate the minds of their employees. Intellectual stimulation includes support and encouragement provided by leaders to members of the team and generate innovative ideas on how to change existing procedures or orders to produce effective results, which will boost employee retention (Tian et al., 2022). Employees are dedicated to their duties and to the organization when treated fairly. Dedication represents employee involvement in the job such that the job becomes a source of pride and motivation (Alam et al., 2021). Leaders have varying management strategies. Leaders need to understand that ethical leadership will create a positive environment in the organization.

Leaders need to implement strategies that promote ethical and moral behavior among employees. Employees model the behavioral pattern of the leader by observing, emulating, and replicating such behavior if found attractive and credible (Babalola et al., 2014). Employees are attracted to a leader who can aid in their development. Leaders are trustworthy, understanding, and fair and will motivate employees to improve productivity. How a leader views an employee is also important. The leader and employee relationship should be considered when articulating employee engagement. Carasco-Saul et al. (2015) confirmed that the way leaders view and are viewed by followers, the degree they influence followers' perceptions, and the quality of the work environment they cultivate can affect the effectiveness of leadership and enhancement of employee engagement.

Ethical leadership increases job satisfaction. Job satisfaction encourages organizational success. Job satisfaction affects employee performance, meaning that an individual's performance will increase when the job satisfaction of individuals is at a high. A person works with passion if satisfaction can be obtained from the work (Atmojo, 2012). Leaders can focus their efforts on moral development by hosting seminars and workshops about ethics. The workshops will be valuable to employees and will benefit the organization. Employees feel appreciated when leaders take the opportunity to assist in employee development.

## Conclusion

The purpose of this qualitative multi case study was to explore successful strategies that business leaders use to motivate employees in their organizations. Participant responses from the face-to-face semi-structured interviews were from leaders who motivated employees by implementing successful ethical management strategies in their company. In addition to the interviews, I reviewed company documents such as policy and procedure manuals, ordinances, and archival information to complement data collection. Information derived from the methodological triangulation data collection process was used to validate data source themes.

Ko's et al. (2017) concept of ethical leadership was used as the conceptual framework for this study. When reviewing the responses from the interviews, two themes were identified (a) leader and employee relationships in the organization and (b) moral and ethical values of a leader. The conceptual framework used and literature reviewed support the findings of this study. Displaying ethical behavior in an organization can have significant benefit to the success of the organization. Employees who work in an organization that is managed by an ethical leader are dedicated and are satisfied with their work environment. The moral traits displayed by the leader is passed on to employees, who use these ethical standards in their everyday life. Effective ethical practices benefit the business and will enable its ability to operate efficiently while developing employees' moral competences in the process.

## THOUGHTS FROM THE ACADEMIC ENTREPRENEUR

*The Problem to be Solved:*
- Some business leaders did not use effective ethical strategies to motivate employees in their organizations.

*The Goals:*
- Understanding ethical strategies business leaders use to motivate their employees while managing the operations of their organizations.

*The Questions to Ask:*
- What does ethical leadership mean as a leader working in the Criminal Justice System?
- What does employee engagement mean to you?
- How do you implement strategies in your organization?
- What ethical strategies do you use to promote a moral environment in your organization?
- How did these strategies assist to motivate employees?
- What information can you share that was not already covered?

*Today's Business Application:*
- By identifying effective ethical strategies that focus on employee engagement, leaders can create a moral environment in the organization. This will aid in the organizational performance and stability of the organization, while contributing to social change.

# REFERENCES

Alam, I., Singh, J., & Islam, M. (2021). Does supportive supervisor complements the effect of ethical leadership on employee engagement? *Cogent Business & Management, 8*(1), 1-15. https://doi.org/10.1080/23311975.2021.1978371

Ashfaq, F., Abid, G., & Ilyas, S. (2021). Effect of ethical leadership on employee engagement: Role of self-efficacy and organizational commitment. *European Journal of Investigation in Health Psychology and Education, 11*, 962-974. https://doi.org/10.3390/ejihpe11030071

Atkin-Plunk, C., & Armstrong, G. (2013). Transformational leadership skills and correlates of prison warden job stress. *Criminal Justice and Behavior, 40*(4), 551-568. https://doi.org/10.1177/0093854812460036

Atmojo, M. (2012). The influence of transformational leadership on job satisfaction, organizational commitment, and employee performance. *International Research Journal of Business Studies, 5*(2), 113-128. https://doi.org/10.21632/irjbs

Avey, J., Wernsing, T., & Palanski, M. (2012). Exploring the process of ethical leadership: The mediating role of employee voice and psychological ownership. *Journal of Business Ethics*. https://doi.org/10.1007/s10551-012-1298-2

Babalola, M., Stouten, J., & Euwema, M. (2014). Frequent change and turnover intention: The moderating role of ethical leadership. *Journal of Business Ethics*. https://doi.org/10.1007/s10551-014-2433-z

Bachmann, B. (2017). *Ethical leadership in organizations concepts and implementation.* Springer International. https://doi.org/10.1007/978-3-319-42942-7

Bavik, Y., Tang, P., Shao, R., & Lam, L. (2017). Ethical leadership and employee knowledge sharing: Exploring dual-mediation paths. *The Leadership Quarterly, 29*(2). 1-14. https://doi.org/10.1016/j.leaqua.2017.05.006

Bedi, A., Alpaslan, C., & Green, S. (2015) A meta-analytic review of ethical leadership outcomes and moderators. *Journal of Business Ethics. 139*, 517-536. https://doi.org/10.1007/s10551-015-2625-1

Branicki, L. (2020). C****: Ethics of care and feminist crisis management. *Gender Work and Organization, 27*, 872-883. https://doi.org/10.1111/gwao.12491

Brown, M. E., Treviño, L. K., & Harrison, D. A. (2005). Ethical leadership: A social learning perspective for construct development and testing. *Organizational Behavior and Human Decision Processes, 97*(2), 117-134. https://doi.org/10.1016/j.obhdp.2005.03.002

Carasco-Saul, M., Kim, W., & Kim, T. (2015). Leadership and employee engagement: proposing research agendas through a review of literature. *Human Resource Development Review, 14*(1), 38-63. https://doi.org/10.1177/1534484314560406

Cockcroft, T. W. (2014) Police culture and transformational leadership: Outlining the contours of a troubled relationship. *Policing: A Journal of Policy and Practice, 8,* 5-13. https://doi.org/10.1093/police/pat040

Downe, J., Cowell, R., & Morgan, K. (2016). What determines ethical behavior in public organizations: Is it rules or leadership? *Public Administration Review, 76*(6), 898-909. https://doi.org/10.1111/puar.12562

Engelbrecht, A. S., Heine, G., & Mahembe, B. (2017). Integrity, ethical leadership, trust, and work engagement. *Leadership & Organization Development Journal, 38*(3), 368-379. https://doi.org/10.1108/LODJ-11-2015-0237

Fehr, R., Yamm, K., & Dang, C. (2015). Moralized leadership: The construction and consequences of ethical leader perceptions. *Academy of Management Review, 40*(2), 182-209. https://doi.org/10.5465/amr.2013.0358

Ferrell, O., Harrison, D., Ferrell, L., & Hair, J. (2019). Business ethics, corporate social responsibility, and brand attitudes: An exploratory study. *Journal of Business Research, 95,* 491-501. https://doi.org/10.1016/j.jbusres.2018.07.039

Halbusi, H., Williams, K. A., Ramayah, T., Aldieri, L., & Vinci, C. P. (2021). Linking ethical leadership and ethical climate to employees' ethical behavior: The moderating role of person-organization fit. *Personnel Review, 50*(1), 159-185. http://doi.org/10.1108/PR-09-2019-0522

Hartog, D. (2015). Ethical leadership. *The Annual Review of Organizational Psychology and Organizational Behavior, 2,* 409-434. https://doi.org/10.1146/annurev-orgpsych-032414-111237

Javed, B., Khan, A., Bashir, S., & Arjoon, S. (2016): Effect of ethical leadership on creativity: The role of psychological empowerment. *Current Issues in Tourism, 20*(8), 839-851. https://doi.org/10.1080/13683500.2016.1188894

Kets de Vries, M., Sexton, J., & Ellen, B. P. (2016). Destructive and transformational leadership in Africa, *African Journal of Management, 2*(2), 166-187. https://doi.org/10.1080/23322373.2016.1175267

Ko, C., Ma, J., Bartnik, R., Haney, M., & Kang, M. (2017). Ethical leadership: An integrative review and future. *Research Agenda, Ethics & Behavior, 28*(2), 104-132. https://doi.org/10.1080/10508422.2017.1318069

Lawton, A., & Pa-ez, I. (2015). Developing a framework for ethical leadership. *Journal of Business Ethics, 130,* 639-649. https://doi.org/10.1007/s10551-014-2244-2

Lazim, N., Salim, N., & Wahab, S. (2020). Low morality among employees due to pandemic C**** and leadership challenge: A literature survey. *Asian Journal of Behavioral Sciences, 2*(4), 26-37. http://myjms.mohe.gov.my/index.php/ajbs

Lei, H., Ha, A. T. L., & Le, P. B. (2020). How ethical leadership cultivates radical and incremental innovation: The mediating role of tacit and explicit knowledge sharing. *Journal of Business & Industrial Marketing, 35*(5), 849-862. https://www.emerald.com/insight/content/doi/10.1108/JBIM-05-2019-0180/full/html

Obama, B. (2017). The president's role in advancing criminal justice reform *U.S. Department of Justice Publications and Materials, 31*. http://digitalcommons@universityofnebraska-lincoln

Ocansey, E., & Ganu, J. (2017). The role of corporate culture in managing occupational fraud. *Research Journal of Finance and Accounting, 8*(24), 102-107. https://core.ac.uk/download/pdf/234632203.pdf

Ozbag, G. (2016). The role of personality in leadership: Five factor personality traits and ethical leadership. *Procedia - Social and Behavioral Sciences, 235*, 235-242. https://doi.org/10.1016/j.sbspro.2016.11.019

Park, E., Kim, K., & Kwon, S. (2017). Corporate social responsibility as a determinant of consumer loyalty: An examination of ethical standard, satisfaction, and trust. *Journal of Business Research, 76*, 8-13. https://doi.org/10.1016/j.jbusres.2017.02.017

Pasricha, P., Singh, B., & Verma, P. (2017). Ethical leadership, organic organizational cultures and corporate social responsibility: An empirical study in social enterprises. *Journal of Business Ethics. 151*, 941-958. https://doi.org/10.1007/s10551-017-3568-5

Perry, J. L., de Graaf, G., van der Wal, Z., & van Montfort, C. (2014). Returning to our roots: "Good government" evolves to "good governance." *Public Administration Review, 74*(1), 27-28. https://www.researchgate.net

Tian, H., Iqbal, S., Akhtar, S., Qalati, S., Anwar, F., & Khan, M. (2022). The effect of transformational leadership on employee retention: Mediation and moderation through organizational citizenship behavior and communication. *Frontiers in Psychology, 11*(314), 1-11. https://doi.org/10.3389/fpsyg.2020.00314

Wenzel, M., & Okimoto, T. (2016). Retributive justice. *Handbook of Social Justice Theory and Research*. Springer. https://doi.org/10.1007/978-1-4939-3216-0

## About the Author...

**Dr. Kevin Grant** is the Operations Manager at the Academy of Sport, University of the West Indies, Cave Hill campus. Before working at the University of the West Indies, he worked at Ernst & Young as a senior auditor. Dr. Kevin completed his Bachelor of Science in Business from the University of Phoenix in 2008. He then enrolled in the University of Wales, where he completed his Master of Business Administration (MBA) in 2011.

Dr. Kevin joined the University of the West Indies in 2013 with a focus of becoming a professor in the field of management and leadership. As Operations Manager, he is responsible for strategic planning and the development of effective systems and processes within the Academy of Sport.

Dr. Kevin is keen on self-development and in sharing knowledge and expertise with his peers. To further develop his skills, he enrolled as a student at Walden University and completed his Doctorate of Business Administration (DBA) in 2019. As a graduate of Walden University, Dr. Kevin sits as a member of the National Society of Leadership and Success, offering expertise in management and leadership strategies to various organizations.

Dr. Kevin has published six chapters and four eBooks on leadership concepts. The latest is *The Effect of Ethical Leadership on Employee Engagement: A Moral Approach to Management* (2023). He received #1 International best seller for his chapters published in The Refractive Thinker series.

To reach **Dr. Kevin Grant** for additional information or guest speaking, please contact him at **e-mail:** kevingrant26@gmail.com

CHAPTER 4

# Smoke and Mirrors— The Illusion of Education in America's Schools: Compulsory Preparation for Incarceration

*Dr. Teresa Sanders*

Dr. Martin Luther King, Jr. stated: "The function of education is to teach one to think intensively and to think critically. Intelligence plus character—that is the goal of true education" (Stanford University, 2023). The use of intelligence and character as measures of education success are fitting, and universally applicable. Social and education equity is inherent as these measures are attainable by people of all races, cultures, and social classes. Expected outcomes can be tailored to any student's needs and abilities and create pathways to productive adulthood for all learners. Productive adults work, build communities, and develop into capable political and business leaders.

Schools in America have the potential to function in, and even surpass, Dr. King's vision of education. American schools have access to fiduciary, technological, academic, human, and other resources needed to ensure students reach optimal social and academic achievement. Yet, past and current education outcomes reveal a persistent substandard performance of America's students in the critical areas of reading and math (National Assessment Governing Board, 2023).

The lackluster performances of America's students raises

concerns that should be red flags for education stakeholders. Taxpayers should want to know why America's students' reading and math performances are persistently substandard, why no effective corrective measures are implemented, who is being held accountable and responsible for the dire education outcomes in America's schools, and why this travesty of failure is allowed to persist. It is important to know who is profiting from allowing this failure to continue.

A refractive thinking approach to education in America's schools is overdue. Education administrators can no longer proceed with the status quo when educating children. The social and fiduciary costs of academic failure to students, taxpayers, communities, and the nation is too great. The future of America and its citizens depends on a comprehensive review of education policies and priorities to ensure education outcomes reflect public education's purpose.

America is considered the most powerful nation in the world (McNeil, 2019). Much of America's powerful perception is related to the country's ability to lead the world economically, technologically, militarily, and academically (McNeil, 2019). America also imprisons more people than any country in the world (World Population Review, 2023). If America is to retain its reputation of perceived power in the world, the education system in America requires an overhaul. If America wants to maintain the designation of the world leader of incarcerated citizens, nothing needs to be changed in America's schools.

## Education in America

### *Early American Education*
In the early 1800s, American education emphasized literacy, social, and functional skills (Urban et al., 2008). Education in America began as a way to ensure members of society learned

the values, social norms, knowledge, and skills needed to develop into productive citizens (University of Minnesota, 2023; Urban et al., 2008). Education attainment was formal in a school setting with a teacher or trained professional and informal, which was at home with parents as teachers (University of Minnesota, 2023).

Parents were required to teach their children to read (University of Minnesota, 2023). While typically not required in the colonies, only one in 10 colonial children attended school (usually wealthy children) while others learned trades (Urban et al., 2008).

In the mid-1800s, the need for compulsory education was established so free, formal education opportunities would be available to all children, not just the wealthy (Urban et al., 2008). Education was compulsory to encourage unity, patriotism, and to teach American values to immigrants (University of Minnesota, 2023). An increasingly industrial economy called for workers with the ability to read, write, and calculate math proficiently, whereas those skills were not as critical in agriculture (University of Minnesota, 2023).

Compulsory education in America had its critics, given that a major reason for its establishment was the cultivation of workers for the expanding industrialization occurring at the time (Bowles & Gintis, 2002; Cole, 2008). The ability to learn and work benefited the learners who were typically poor, but it also served wealthy business owners by supplying much needed laborers for their businesses, positively affecting productivity and profitability (Bowles & Gintis, 2002).

The same criticism of contemporary education in America could be made in 2023. Students must attend school to gain the skills needed to function as productive adults in society. Critical components of contemporary education such as literacy and math competency (Wakelyn, 2022) and social and functional skills continue to decline (Russo & Bonner, 2021) raising concerns of why

American students attending school and what future we prepare students for.

America's school system has a reputation of being among the best school systems in the world, ranking at #14 out of 73 countries (U.S. News & Reports, 2023). Students with disabilities or from low socioeconomic circumstances have federally mandated support available to help them be successful in school and life (U.S. Department of Education, 2023). Access to education technology and internet connectivity are increasingly available to low socioeconomic circumstances, rural, and displaced students, often free of charge (U.S. Department of Agriculture, 2021).

Public education in America is supported by taxpayers, philanthropic groups (Philanthropy News Digest, 2006), teacher unions (Association of Texas Professional Educators, 2023) and politicians (Svitek, 2022). Efforts to redirect public education resources to private or homeschooling options are vigorously contested (Bedrick & Tarnowski, 2021). Public schools are a fiercely protected entity; however, a review of past and current education statistics suggested the quality of education in America is nothing more than an illusion. Taxpayer funded slight-of-hand: smoke and mirrors.

### Student Achievement

Adult productivity is among the primary reasons for compulsory education in America (Urban et al., 2008). The ability to read, write, calculate math, and think critically (Monych, 2023) are minimal skills needed to function, work, and conduct business effectively (King, 2018; Thakkar, 2023). Additional knowledge of social studies, science, history, and the arts are necessary to complete college studies. Social, functional, and coping skills are necessary to thrive in the home, on the job, and in society (Thakkar, 2023). According to education data, America's schools are not teaching or reinforcing the skills and knowledge necessary to accomplish public education's stated goals (Russo & Bonner, 2020).

According to current and germinal student performance statistics, America's public education system has persisted in a state of failure for decades (National Assessment Governing Board, 2023). Academic failure leads to increases in criminal behavior and incarceration (Bureau of Justice Statistics, 2008; Prison Policy Initiative, 2022). Low literacy and illiteracy are causes of academic failure (Prison Policy Initiative, 2022). Education attainment is an effective way to reduce the number of incarcerated people in America and concurrently save billions of taxpayers' dollars spent on loss of productivity and criminal justice related costs (National Dropout Prevention Center, 2022).

## Academics

The National Assessment of Educational Progress (NAEP) is a widely administered education assessment mandated by congress. The National Center for Education Statistics (NCES, 2023) administers the test. The reading and math assessment occurs every 2 years at grades 4, 8, and 12. Science and writing are assessed every 4 years. The assessment gauges the academic progress of America's students in each respective subject area (National Center for Education Statistics [NCES], 2023).

## Literacy Outcomes

According to the results of the 2022 NAEP, almost 70% of America's 4th grade students cannot read proficiently, which is up from 66% in 2019. The term *proficient* is defined as showing competency over rigorous or challenging content, including knowledge of subject-matter, the ability to apply the knowledge in real-life situations and possessing the skills needed to analyze information (National Assessment Governing Board, 2023). Reading scores for 4th and 8th grade students are down from the previous assessment in 2019 (NCES, 2023).

Fourth grade reading scores in 2022 were lower than assessment years back to 2005 (National Assessment Governing Board, 2023). Fourth grade scores in 2022 were not significantly better than performance scores 30 years ago in 1992 (National Assessment Governing Board, 2023). Fourth grade performance scores are significant because reading instruction transitions to reading application at the end of 3rd grade. In 3rd grade, students are *learning to read*. In 4th grade, students are *reading to learn*.

Students who lack the ability to read proficiently by the end of 3rd grade are statistically unlikely to catch up and are at higher risk of dropping out of school before graduating (Christeson et al., 2008). Dropout rates are tied to crime, criminal justice contacts, and incarceration among other social problems (Bureau of Justice Statistics, 2008; Christeson et al., 2008; Prison Policy Initiative, 2022).

In 2022, reading performances for 8th graders were similar to those of the 4th graders. Eighth grade reading scores in 2022 were lower than reading assessment scores dating back to 1998. Like the 4th grade reading scores, 8th grade performance scores were not significantly better than they were in 1992.

Reading proficiency is foundational to student achievement. Illiteracy is a primary risk factor for incarceration (Christeson et al., 2008; Prison Policy Initiative, 2022). Given the financial and other resources available to America's schools and students, 30 years of stagnant literacy achievement scores indicate a major problem in the system. The persistent underperformance of America's students should be cause for alarm to education stakeholders.

**Student Dropouts**

Students who drop out of high school are almost four times more likely to be arrested and more than 10 times more likely to go to prison compared to their peers who graduate (Christeson et al., 2008). Every class of dropouts costs the nation $200 billion through lost wages and income taxes that subsequently could not be collected (Prison Policy Initiative, 2022). Low literacy and illiteracy influence the student dropout rate in the United States. Dropout status is a critical risk factor for future incarceration (Prison Policy Initiative, 2022). Supporting student success and graduation would reduce spending on incarceration and boost the economy by recapturing billions of lost tax dollars resulting from dropouts going to prison instead of going to work (Prison Policy Initiative, 2022).

## *Illiteracy in America*

Literacy includes the definition as the ability to understand and use information from text in all written formats (NCES, 2003). As of 2023, 21% of the more than 300 million American adults are illiterate (Rothwell, 2020) costing the United States about $2.2 trillion annually (Think Impact, 2023). More than 130 million adults in America have low literacy skills, meaning they are reading below a 6th-grade level (Rothwell, 2020). Illiteracy and low literacy among adults negatively affect individuals, communities, and the economy (Diallo, 2020). Illiteracy and low literacy limit one's employment opportunities, leads to increased poverty, crime, and reduces one's life expectancy (Diallo, 2020). Ending illiteracy would have a positive impact on the U.S. economy (Rothwell, 2020).

Literacy is divided into six levels, starting with *Below Level 1,* which represents basic vocabulary knowledge but lacking understanding of sentences and paragraphs (National Literacy Trust, 2017). At the fifth and highest level of literacy, adults can competently locate, incorporate, and synthesize a variety of text, understand rhetoric, infer, detect subtleties, use evidence to support arguments, apply specialized knowledge in circumstances, and other related skills (National Literacy Trust, 2017).

Rothwell (2020) suggested if all adults in America could read at level 3 competency, an additional $2.2 trillion worth of income would be generated in the United States. Two trillion dollars is equivalent to 10% of the nation's gross domestic product (GDP). The fiduciary benefit of literacy alone should be motivation for improving academic outcomes in our nation's schools. Given the number of illiterate adults in America, and the correlation between illiteracy and crime, it is not surprising that the United States incarcerates more adults than any other country in the world. With only 25% of 4th graders reading proficiently and just 10 years before they become adults, the illiteracy statistics in America will continue to deteriorate.

## *Illiteracy and Criminal Justice*

Illiteracy and incarceration are directly connected (Bureau of Justice Statistics, 2003; Christeson et al., 2008; Diallo, 2020; Prison Policy Initiative, 2022). The outcomes of illiteracy and academic failure are devastating and provide a path to prison for many students, particularly African American students (Bureau of Justice Statistics, 2008; Prison Policy Initiative, 2022).

In the United States, 70% of incarcerated adults and 85% of youth in the juvenile court system are functionally illiterate (Bureau of Justice Statistics, 2003; Prison Policy Initiative, 2022). These numbers represent the inability to read, but they also represent the inability to effectively problem-solve, access information, participate politically, communicate, think critically, pursue higher education, and reap the benefits of a vibrant economy (Kohlenberg, 2020).

The United States has the highest incarceration rate in the world, and one of the highest recidivism rates (National Institute of Justice, 2023). Recidivism is determined by additional criminal behavior that causes a person to be rearrested, convicted, or sent back to prison within 3 years of release (National Institute of

Justice, 2023). In 2023, 44% of inmates in America are reincarcerated within their first year out of prison (National Institute of Justice, 2023). The term *mass incarceration* is used to describe high rates of incarceration of youth and adults (Brennan Center for Justice, 2018). America's justice system practices mass incarceration but neglects to develop effective programs and plans to reduce recidivism (National Institute of Justice, 2023). Perhaps the absence of effective rehabilitation plans explains why the recidivism rate in America is so high. Taxpayers are spending more than $40,000 per year, per inmate in America's federal prisons and anywhere from $14,000 to $70,000 annually to incarcerate an inmate at the state level (Interrogating Justice, 2023).

## Investing in Reading Instruction and Remediation

Effective, early reading instruction and remediation is foundational to reducing and ideally eliminating illiteracy and academic failure in our nation's schools (National Literacy Trust, 2017). The cost of effective reading instruction and remediation is negligible compared to the costs associated with incarcerating an individual for a year. In a study titled "Cost-Effectiveness Analysis of Early Reading Programs: A Demonstration with Recommendations for Future Research," researchers calculated the cost of seven effective reading programs designed for struggling or low readers in kindergarten, 1st, and 3rd grades. The programs reviewed included K-PALS, Steppingstones, Sound Partners, Fast ForWord Reading, Corrective Reading, Reading Recovery, and Wilson Reading System (Holland et al., 2015). Each program effectively improved academic outcomes in at least one of the areas of fluency, letter recognition, or comprehension (Holland et al., 2015).

## Costs Per Student

The cost to execute each program was divided equally across the number of students participating to determine the per student cost. Other factors such as the length of remediation and whether the program was core instruction or supplemental also affected per student costs (National Literacy Trust, 2017). The range of costs per student was as low as $282 per student for Steppingstones and up to $10,000 per student for Corrective Reading (Holland et al., 2015)

Program cost increased significantly with each higher grade level. Increasing costs should serve as encouragement for school districts to address reading difficulties early and rigorously to simultaneously reduce remediation costs, and decrease illiteracy and the negative social and economic outcomes associated with reading failure. Even at the highest cost of reading remediation at $10,000 for the Corrective Reading program, the per person cost of incarceration is significantly more at $14,000 on the low end and up to $70,000 on the high end (Interrogating Justice, 2023).

*Public Education Agenda*

The resistance of federal education administrators in America to invest more time and financial resources into programs and services that can improve literacy and reduce criminal justice and incarceration costs is not apparent. Reading attainment and remediation costs less initially and can potentially reap billions of dollars long term by reducing spending on criminal justice matters and incarceration (Rothwell, 2020). The efforts to address illiteracy in America's schools has been limited to empty political promises, ineffective instruction in classrooms, and the expenditure of tax dollars on what we know is not working to improve student literacy.

The *prison industrial complex* refers to the web of legislators, companies, investors, and government systems invested in policing, surveillance and construction of prisons (Tufts University, 2023). Many of those in the web have overlapping or conflicting interests and profit from mass incarceration (Tufts University,

2023). Private prisons are run with little oversight or regulation allowing them to cut maintenance, medical services, and food to increase profitability (Tufts University, 2023). In 2019, approximately 49% of state and federal inmates were in state-run facilities while 51% were housed in private facilities (Maruschak & Buehler, 2021).

Education stakeholders could justifiably question the purpose of compulsory education in America. The nation's schools are not a place where youth are developing into literate, responsible, critical thinkers who will be prepared to compete in the workplace and participate competently in political processes. America's future business, agricultural, and political leaders are not on their way to their roles as leaders in America. American taxpayers are not reaping a quality return from the billions of dollars spent on education in America. Perhaps the purpose of the nation's schools is to produce and reproduce generations of inmates to fuel America's current and future mass incarceration economy.

## Conclusion

Despite the decades of data highlighting, the correlation between education failure and incarceration, federal education administrators in the United States have yet to implement a plan of correction that changes the negative trajectory of America's schools and the subsequent effect it will have on communities, the economy, and the lives of those failed by the education system. Those responsible for correction are unable or *unwilling* to correct this persistent problem.

The problem of academic failure in America's schools appears to be allowed to persist intentionally. Methods to address this failure and correct the problem are immediately available at far less social and fiduciary cost than the personal and social consequences of academic failure. All education stakeholders must demand accountability and correction in the nation's education system if America is to prepare its youth to lead future social, political, and economic progression.

To continue to ignore this phenomenon provides America's students first-class tickets to the pipeline to prison and ensures the United States will lack a suitable workforce to compete in the global business, political, and academic environments. A refractive thinking approach to literacy and education could change the failing trajectory of education in America and subsequently improve lives, communities, and the economy.

Prioritizing literacy and reading remediation early and rigorously in schools would reduce the academic failure that fuels the Criminal Justice System and mass incarceration. Money that is not spent on criminal justice matters can be redirected to programs where illiterate adults and children have opportunities to receive remediation at any age. The fiscal enrichment of the mass incarceration market would decline but the quality of life for those who are illiterate, would-be inmates, and American taxpayers could improve significantly.

## THOUGHTS FROM THE ACADEMIC ENTREPRENEUR

*The Problems to be Solved:*

- More than 20% of American adults are illiterate.
- In America's schools, almost 70% of students are illiterate, costing American taxpayers billions of dollars annually through criminal justice, incarceration costs, and loss revenue.
- The human costs of illiteracy and incarceration are incalculable.

*The Goals:*

- To prioritize addressing reading attainment and remediation early and effectively to reduce illiteracy and the incarceration rates in the United States.

*The Questions to be Asked:*

- Given the human, social and fiduciary costs related to criminal justice and incarceration, why isn't literacy attainment a priority in America's schools?

*Today's Business Application:*

- Making literacy an immediate and ongoing priority in America can improve lives, schools, communities, and the economy ensuring that America's future workforce can compete effectively in global social, business, and political matters.

# REFERENCES

Association of Texas Professional Educators. (2023). *Education.* https://www.atpe.org/

Bedrick, J., & Tarnowski, E. (2021). *Who's afraid of school choice? Examining the validity and intensity of predictions by school choice opponents.* EdChoice. https://files.eric.ed.gov/fulltext/ED615891.pdf

Bowles, S., & Gintis, H. (2002). Schooling in capitalist America revisited. *Sociology of Education, 75*(1), 1-18. https://doi.org/10.2307/3090251

Brennan Center for Justice. (2023, March 20). *The history of mass incarceration.* http://Brennancenter.org/our-work/analysis-opinion/histoy-mass-incarceration

Bureau of Justice Statistics. (2008). *Education and correctional populations.* Bureau of Justice Statistics Special Report. https://bjs.ojp.gov/content/pub/pdf/ecp.pdf

Cole, M. (2008). *Marxism and educational theory: Origins and issues.* Routledge.

Christeson, B., Lee, B., Schafer, S., Kass, D., & Messner-Zidell, S. (2008). *School or the streets. Crime and America's dropout crisis.* Alabama Partnership for Children. https://alabamapartnershipforchildren.org/wp-content/uploads/2016/12/School-or-the-Streets-Crime-and-Americas-Dropout-Crisis.pdf

Diallo, A. (2020). *Improving illiteracy in the United States: Recommendations for increasing reading success.* Center for American Progress. https://www.americanprogress.org/

Interrogating Justice. (2023). *Annual prison costs going into 2023.* https://interrogatingjustice.org/

King, A. (2018). *Reading and writing in the math classroom.* Edutopia. https://www.edutopia.org/

Kohlenberg, M. (2020). Booked but can't read: "functional literacy," national citizenship, and the new face of Dred Scott in the age of mass incarceration. *NYU Review of Law and Social Change, 44*(213). https://socialchangenyu.com/wp-content/uploads/2020/05/Mckenna-Kohlenberg_RLSC_Volume44.Issue2_-1.pdf

Maruschak, L., & Buehler, E. (2023). *Census of state and federal adult correctional facilities, 2019-statistical tables.* Bureau of Justice Statistics. https://bjs.ojp.gov

McNeil, T. (2019). *Why the United States is the only superpower.* Tufts Now. https://now.tufts.edu/

Monych, B. (2023). *Critical thinking skills and how to develop them in employees.* Inspirity. https://www.insperity.com/

National Assessment Governing Board. (2023). *What are NAEP achievement levels and how are they determined?* https://www.nagb.gov/

National Center for Education Statistics (NCES). (2003). *Adult literacy and life skills survey.* https://nces.ed.gov/

National Center for Education Statistics (NCES). (2023) *What PIAAC measures.* https://nces.ed.gov/

National Dropout Prevention Center (2022). *Administrators toolkit.* https://dropoutprevention.org/resources/statistics/quick-facts/economic-impacts-of-dropouts/

National Institute of Justice. (2023). *Recidivism.* https://nij.ojp.gov/topics/corrections/recidivism

National Literacy Trust. (2017). *What do adult literacy levels mean?* https://literacytrust.org.uk/

Prison Policy Initiative. (2022). *Unites States Profile.* https://www.prisonpolicy.org/

Rothwell, J. (2020). *Assessing the economic gains of eradicating illiteracy nationally and regionally in the United States.* The Barbara Bush Foundation for Family Literacy. https://www.barbarabush.org/

Philanthropy News Digest. (2006). *Texas public schools turn to education foundations.* https://philanthropynewsdigest.org/news/texas-public-schools-turn-to- education-foundations

Russo, D., & Bonner T. (2021). *Why schools don't have time to teach social skills.* Buffalo State University. https://digitalcommons.buffalostate.edu/srcc-sp20-edu/23/

Stanford University. (2023). *The purpose of education.* https://kinginstitute.stanford.edu/king-papers/documents/purpose-education

Svitek, P. (2022). *With rural Texas watching, Greg Abbott and Beto O'Rourke dig in on school vouchers fight.* The Texan Tribune. https://www.texastribune.org/

Thakkar, J. (2023). *Why prioritizing soft skills in hiring is crucial to the modern workplace.* Entrepreneur. https://www.entrepreneur.com/

Think Impact. (2023). *Literacy statistics.* https://www.thinkimpact.com/literacy-statistics/

Tufts University. (2023). *What is the Prison Industry Complex?* https://sites.tufts.edu/prisondivestment/the-pic-and-mass-incarceration/

University of Minnesota. (2023). *A brief history of education in America.* https://open.lib.umn.edu/

Urban, W. J., Jennings L., & Wagoner, J. (2008). *American education: A history* (4th ed.). Routledge.

U.S. Department of Agriculture. (2021). *USDA to make up to 1.5 billion available to help people living in rural communities access high speed internet.* https://www.rd.usda.gov/

U.S. Department of Education. (2023). *IDEA.* https://sites.ed.gov/idea/

U.S. News and World Report (2023). *The best countries for education.* https://www.usnews.com/news/best-countries/best-countries-for-education

Wakelyn, D. S. (2022). *Middle school math needs to be every superintendent's priority.* EdSource.

https://edsource.org/2022/middle-school-math-needs-to-be-every-superintendents-new-priority/680548

World Population Review. (2023). *Incarceration rates by country.* https://worldpopulationreview.com/

## *About the Author...*

**Dr. Teresa Sanders** spent 20 years working in mental health/social services in California, before relocating to Texas in 2005. She has been an educator for 17 years, most of which was spent teaching in the public school system. Dr. Teresa is also a six-time international bestselling author. She is a supporter of school choice and facilitates workshops for those considering homeschooling their children or starting a small school.

Dr. Teresa is the owner and founder of Safari Small Schools in Canton, Texas. Safari Small Schools is a five-student, micro-school designed to meet the needs of students who are not thriving in the traditional classroom. Safari Small Schools is successful and is being considered as a model for education services in Kenya.

Dr. Teresa has presented at several international education conferences, where she shares insight and information related to working effectively with the most marginalized students and their families. She is an outspoken advocate helping families navigate special education and other school-related services. Dr. Teresa serves as an education resource in the community and is involved in literacy attainment for children and adults. On a personal note, Dr. Teresa is married with one adult child and enjoys rural living. She is an avid traveler having visited 36 countries on three continents with a goal of traveling the world.

To reach **Dr. Teresa Sanders** for public speaking, consulting or a friendly chat by email or phone, please visit her **website:** http://www.SafariSmallSchools.com or **e-mail:** DrSanders@SafariSmallSchools.com **Phone:** (469) 360-8528

CHAPTER 5

# Leaders in American Institutions: Affecting Change for Diversity, Equity, and Inclusion

## Dr. Anita A. Francis & Dr. Paula Schuh Berbeco

*"If one really wishes to know how justice is administered in a country, one does not question the policemen, the lawyers, the judges, or the protected members of the middle class. One goes to the unprotected – those, precisely, who need the law's protection most! – and listen to their testimony ... It is certain, in any case, that ignorance, allied with power, is the most ferocious enemy justice can have."*

—JAMES BALDWIN

Diversity, Equity, and Inclusion (DE&I) as a societal, institutional, and organizational phenomenon remains a ubiquitous challenge for leaders (Francis, 2022a). DE&I issues are pervasive in American institutions, including the Criminal Justice System (Lang & Spitzer, 2020; Smedley, 2007). DE&I covers broad topics such as inclusive cultures, leadership, discrimination, and unconscious bias (Grissom, 2018). Diversity may include gender, race, ethnicity, religion, nationality, sexual orientation, veterans, people with disabilities, religion, place of practice, and practice type (Grissom, 2018; Tan, 2019). Equity ensures all individuals have access to the same opportunities to gain experience, contribute, and develop in the workplace regardless of identity (Tan, 2019). The process of being equitable begins by acknowledging the unequal starting point and working towards correcting and addressing the imbalance (Tan, 2019). Inclusion refers to the intentional, ongoing efforts to make sure diverse people with different identities can participate in every aspect of the work in an organization, including leadership positions and decision-making processes (Tan, 2019; Taylor, 2020). Inclusion refers to how diverse individuals are valued as respected members and how they are welcomed in an organization, project, or social system (Tan, 2019; Taylor, 2020).

Refractive Thinkers are needed to apply new concepts for meaningful change to organizational and institutional DE&I challenges (Francis, 2022b). Refractive Thinkers apply strategies to push cognitive thinking and boundaries beyond conventional practices (McKay, 2022). Getting to a new paradigm of thought requires understanding the contributing tensions and gaps of DE&I in institutions. Our chapter begins with the influence of American history and the interdependency of institutions that contributed to systemic DE&I challenges. We will discuss how organizational culture and leaders can positively affect and improve DE&I.

## The Influence of American History

DE&I is a complex phenomenon with roots deeply buried in American culture and nurtured by generational experiences. Traditionalist and Baby Boomer generational views about DE&I are shaped by their social upbringing and the events they experienced at the macro and micro levels. Traditionalists were born between 1925 and 1945, and Baby Boomers were born between 1946 and 1964 (Darby & Morrell, 2019). These generations experienced social and institutional segregation in the housing, education, financial, workplace, and Criminal Justice Systems. Segregation set people apart based on their identity or affiliation, such as White or Black race characterizations. The collective structural advantages, including financial, legal, social, or cultural freedoms to some and not others, are known as *privilege* (Borell et al., 2018), where most of the population is Caucasian and holds the decision-making power in institutions. *White privilege* is an unearned and largely unrecognized benefit (Waite & Nardi, 2021).

Years of operating in homogeneous environments created opportunities of entitlement that have been handed down from generation to generation and translated into White privilege. Some minority Baby Boomers are the descendants of enslaved people and are still fighting for the rights promulgated through the Civil Rights Act of 1964 and landmark cases such as Brown vs. Board of Education (Miller et al., 2021; Scott, 2021). Jim Crow laws passed by previous generations influenced current and future generations (Halloran, 2018). The decision to exclude people of color was enforced by U.S. laws, rules, and regulations, which became the culture and structure of the nation (Halloran, 2018; Scott, 2021). The court's historic ruling of Brown v. Board of Education in 1954 was not the end of school segregation; instead, the ruling was the beginning of a long and challenging struggle to unwind centuries of systemic inequality that has influenced every aspect of American life (Scott, 2021). These historic hurts and disparities must not be forgotten but confronted (Halloran, 2018; Scott, 2021).

Variances in the institutional or societal privilege of minorities went beyond racial or ethnic characteristics and included other marginalized groups. One example is individuals identifying as lesbian, gay, bisexual, transgender, queer, intersex, and asexual (LGBTQIA) (Dawson, 2018). Unlike people with recognizable outward appearances, LGBTQIA individuals could hide behind a silent or unknown identity, culminating in generational cohorts labeled as the Invisible Generation, representing babies born before 1934, and the Silenced Generation, born between 1935 and 1949 (Goldsen et al., 2022). Regardless of outward appearance or silent identities, marginalized and minority groups have systemically been treated differently. Intersectionality, which considers more than one identity, such as being Black or female, contributes to an increased chance of discriminatory behavior, such as racism and sexism (Baum, 2021).

Revisiting American history gives an understanding of how institutions that support social systems contribute to the inclusion or exclusion of minorities. The systemic problem of excluding minorities should be viewed through a social lens, not as isolated cases (Ifekwunigwe et al., 2017; Smedley, 2007; Williams & Smedley, 1994). A review of the organizational literature on workplace DE&I indicated that inclusion does not exist in a vacuum and cannot be managed as such (Johnson et al., 2020; Lang & Spitzer, 2020). When examining techniques leaders used to manage diverse teams in their organizations, one researcher identified the theme of historical tension tightly embedded in American culture and institutions (Francis, 2022a). The phenomenon of race is observed in the interplay of behaviors across institutions. The same historic underpinnings and conundrum of DE&I themes seen in the workplace are also evident in the Criminal Justice System.

## Systemic Institutional Interdependency

Organizational leaders continue to struggle with DE&I since institutional settings do not operate in isolation; they are systemic and interconnected (Francis, 2022a; Lang & Spitzer, 2020). Collective practices in institutions cross over and reinforce similar behaviors. These collective practices and behaviors can cause pervasive inequalities and racial disparities within the labor market, education, criminal justice, health, and housing markets (Lang

& Spitzer, 2020). The same disparity was seen in the Criminal Justice System, especially for imprisonment.

Nationally Black Americans are incarcerated at nearly five times the rate, or more, of White Americans. There was a disproportionate share of Black and Latinx compared to White prisoners (Rezal, 2021). In 2019, the belief that Whites were treated better by police was reported more often by Black (n = 84%) than by White (n = 63%) adults (The National Association for the Advancement of Colored People [NAACP], 2023). Black (n = 65%) and Latinx (n=35%) adults felt targeted because of their race (NAACP, 2023). Black adults (n = 84%) said the Criminal Justice System was more unjust towards Black adults versus White adults (n = 61%) (NAACP, 2023). Increased incarceration of minorities contributed to a lack of participation and presence in the educational system, housing, and financial markets, causing individual, familial, and generational hardships. Legal restrictions against people with arrests and convictions block access to jobs, housing, and educational opportunities (NAACP, 2023). The excessive disparity in incarcerated minorities has a ripple effect on different institutions in the United States. In 34 states, people on parole or probation cannot vote (NAACP, 2023). In 12 states, a felony conviction meant never voting again (NAACP, 2023). Prior incarceration negatively influenced the ability of individuals to obtain federal benefits or get a job (NAACP, 2023).

The lack of participation or community engagement of minorities because of incarceration, the hardship of integrating into society, and the distaste of the Criminal Justice System can further hinder minorities from being represented in the workforce in American organizations and institutions. During research interviews with leaders of diverse teams, participants familiar with the legal system expressed concern that, while there was an increase in female attorneys in the workforce, the numbers were still considerably low for Black males (Francis, 2022a). Black males were graduating from law school at historically higher levels but their presence in the courtrooms was significantly lower than Black females and their White male and female counterparts (Francis, 2022a).

A report by the American Bar Association (ABA) (2022) confirmed that 61% of lawyers are male and 38% are females. For the past 11 years, there has been a decline in ABA-accredited law school enrollment for males from 78,516 in 2010 to 52,058 in 2021. The number of females attending law school increased over the past 5 years from 55,766 in 2016 to 64,861 in 2021 (ABA, 2022). Statistical data collected in 2022 confirmed there is an overrepresentation of White people in the legal profession compared to their presence in the general population (ABA, 2022). Lawyers of color only represented 19% of the population in 2022 compared to 81% of White lawyers (ABA, 2022). Asian, Native American, African American, Hispanic, and mixed races contributed 19% of all U.S. lawyers in 2022 (ABA, 2022). Asian Americans comprise 5.5% of lawyers and 5.9% of the U.S. population (ABA, 2022). Mixed-race lawyers comprise 2.7% of lawyers, aligning with their representative share of the U.S. population of 2.8%. There are 4.5% of African Americans lawyers, although they comprised 13.4% of the U.S. population (ABA, 2022). Hispanics made up 5.8% of lawyers but represented only 18.5% of the general population (ABA, 2022). In 2022, Whites comprised 81% of lawyers, although as a demographic, represented only 60.1% of the U.S. population (ABA, 2022). Judges have the same racial and ethnic disparity. In 2022, 20 states had no judges identifying as a person of color in the highest courts (ABA, 2022). There were no Black judges in 28 states, no Hispanic judges in 39 states, no Asian American judges in 43 states, and no Native American judges in 47 states. Diversity was added when new State Supreme Court Justices took office between April 2021 and May 2022 (ABA, 2022). Fifteen of the 25 new judges were women, 10 were people of color, and out of the 10, seven were women of color (ABA, 2022).

Researchers outlined the historic contributions to systemic inequity and the interconnectedness between institutions. Criminal justice workforce data outlines racial and minority disparity of treatment. The statistics reflect a need for institutional reform and retraining. Making significant strides in DE&I requires Refractive Thinkers to holistically question and evaluate social structures, generational influences, and biases. Leveraging organizational cultures and leaders is one way to support and affect change.

## Organizational Culture and Leaders Supporting DE&I

As organizations become more intentional in DE&I strategies, leaders need to evaluate and be aware of historical or systemic inequities and advocate for improvements in the culture. Creating and sustaining a culture of DE&I is more than a feel-good cause. Organizations benefit from a culture supportive of a diverse and engaged workforce. Diverse employees bring different skills and perspectives that can differentiate one company from another. Diversity can improve a firm's financial performance and stock market reactions and can provide a service or product that meets the needs of a diverse customer base (Berbeco et al., 2022; Lambert, 2016; Pichler et al., 2017).

Employees who can be themselves and freely interact with others contribute to organizational creativity and knowledge (Lambert, 2016). Organizational success or failure can depend on employees' satisfaction and motivation (Francis, 2022a; Sharma et al., 2020). Reaching the pinnacle of human contribution within a sustainable and inclusive workspace starts with meeting fundamental human needs (Cherry, 2021). American psychologist Abraham Maslow (1971) developed a theory explaining how meeting basic needs culminates in self-actualization from a psychological context. Self-actualization is comparable with indicators such as a state of well-being, life satisfaction, and authenticity (Berbeco et al., 2022; Fletcher & Everly, 2021).

Maslow's (1971) hierarchy of needs theory can be applied to employees in an organization. When people feel safe, secure, included, and valued, their self-esteem is bolstered. Employees feel a sense of personal accomplishment in reaching their full potential (Berbeco et al., 2022; Cherry, 2021; Francis, 2022a; Soni & Soni, 2016). When employees' internal and external needs are met, the results are an engaged workforce who feel valued and can bring their best selves to work (Berbeco, 2022; Delaney & Royal, 2017). Workers can be autonomously motivated when an organization aligns with values they can endorse, such as DE&I, the environment, and human rights (Rigby & Ryan, 2018). When minorities are not represented, included, or protected within social structures and institutions, their basic needs are unmet (Cherry, 2021; Francis, 2022a; Sharma et al., 2020; Stewart et al., 2018).

As the workforce becomes more diverse, organizations must apply diversity initiatives to support the workforce's demographic paradigm shift (Deloitte, 2021; Grissom, 2018). Changing the culture and behavior in organizations starts with the leaders. Leaders championing and pioneering DE&I in organizations have realized how challenging it can be, which results in burn out (Baum, 2021). Leaders need resources, training, and organizational support. One qualitative research study interviewed managers leading diverse teams (Francis, 2022a; Francis, 2022b). Leaders reported being encouraged by changes in DE&I but had challenges. The identified themes from the interviews included challenges related to diverse employees, building relationships, having sensitive conversations, identifying bias and discrimination, and having adequate diversity training based on behavioral sciences. Other themes identified from the interviews included the need to reform the role of human resources (HR) and establish DE&I departments. These departments can assist with the other themes identified by leaders, such as hiring, retaining diverse employees, and the lack of minorities in leadership roles (Francis, 2022a). For the latter theme, it was recognized that the workforce could be more equally diverse throughout all levels of the organization. Minorities were concentrated in the lower-paying roles, with little to no decision-making authority (Francis, 2022a).

For leaders to support DE&I, especially those in the White majority, the need to recognize that racism exists because the harsh truth of its existence has not been fully addressed (Baum, 2021). It is natural for humans to avoid or deny painful history or racist actions of violence and discrimination, especially if perceived as not one's problem or experience (Baum, 2021). Trauma in society and the workplace is real and negatively affects individuals and organizations. The implications of minorities being socially excluded have far-reaching effects that span generations resulting in historical trauma (Halloran, 2018; Ifekwunigwe et al., 2017; Scott, 2021; Smedley, 2007). Historical trauma is cumulative, emotional, and psychological wounding over a lifespan and across generations, emanating from massive group experiences (Williams-Washington & Mills, 2018). Minorities continue to experience the trauma of exclusion and alienation (Halloran, 2018; Kossek & Buzzanell, 2018). In the workplace, gender and racial discrimination influence employees' satisfaction, motivation, commitment, enthusiasm, and stress levels (Zia et al., 2020).

Once acknowledging racism and trauma, organizational leaders should offer words of support and show action. Leaders can be valuable representatives of an organization, and research indicated a positive correlation between an individual's leader and the well-being of an individual identifying as a minority (Berbeco, 2022; Berbeco et al., 2022). The dialogue generated by the willingness to listen and absorb feedback from individuals break down barriers. Breaking down barriers is important as tensions from DE&I that result from weak interactions among diverse groups cross U.S. organizations, industries, and sectors (Bernstein et al., 2020; Francis, 2022a). The productive exchanges between individuals, leaders, and team members are encouraged through supportive organizational policies, human resource management strategies, business resource groups, cultural training, facilitation of cultural receptiveness to divergent backgrounds, and effective management (Lambert, 2016; Sharma et al., 2020).

Business resource groups are created at organizations for minority members and allies to represent workers (McNulty et al., 2018). Leaders of diverse teams interviewed by Francis (2022a, 2022b) discussed how their organizations encouraged and incorporated Business Resource Groups (BRGs) to support diverse employees or assist the majority group in understanding the nuances regarding different races and cultures. Further benefits derived from the BRGs are support for diverse employees, assistance in creating an organizational culture and structure that support all groups, and insight into services to multicultural customers (Francis, 2022a; Francis, 2022b). Organizational benefits of creativity and knowledge are reached when diverse individuals feel safe and supported to be themselves and freely interact with others (Lambert, 2016). The multi-level interactions between diverse individuals and groups results in improved organizational creativity, innovation, and performance (Lambert, 2016). A culture of diversity in organizations allows employees to bring their authentic selves to work in an environment that is receptive to all groups (Bourke & Titus, 2019).

Once leaders are aware that diverse team members may have different personal and systemic experiences, and the culture supports the success of diverse teams, the next step is applying leadership styles and skills that support an inclusive work environment (Francis, 2022a). The new psychology of leadership, a concept created by Haslam et al. (2020), provides insight into the new paradigm of leading diverse teams. The new psychology of leadership proposes that effective leaders are those who become a part of the group and represent the group yet lead with their own strengths and character traits. The group influences each other and has a social identity together. The synergy culminates in the unity between the leader and the followers providing transformational collective power (Haslam et al., 2020). Haslam et al.'s (2020) concepts are important to understanding how leaders can engage diverse individuals nationally and globally. In traditional and homogeneous work environments, worldviews and culture are shared, leading to shared assumptions among leaders and followers. In a culturally diverse environment, the leader must facilitate the creation of a shared identity with the different assumptions, backgrounds, cultures, and perspectives. The dynamics influence the leader to create, lead, and harness the collective transformative power (Haslam et al., 2020). Along with creating the team's identity, the organization's culture must also support the team's diversity.

Leaders have an opportunity to make a significant contribution to DE&I efforts by being Refractive Thinkers and seeking alternative solutions to bring about change. Leaders must be transformative and transformable to manage diverse teams (Francis, 2022a; Francis, 2022b). They must consider the system they are operating within, the people in that system and the external environment that will influence the people and the system (Thoroughgood et al., 2018). According to Sharma et al. (2020), how people view their manager's leadership could vary with diverse cultures. Leaders need to take a scientific approach when managing diverse teams. They must draw from various disciplines such as sociology, psychology, and the other behavioral sciences to lead diverse teams and create healthy work environments.

## Conclusion

Historical laws, policies, regulations, and generational biases have their roots deeply entwined in American institutions causing inequality and disadvantages for minorities. This DE&I phenomenon spans American justice, educational, financial, housing, political, and organizational institutions. Psychological trauma can be at the forefront as minorities struggle to exist in environments structured to accommodate the upward mobility of one race over another. A toxic work environment often results in leaders who feel challenged in managing diverse teams, minority employees who feel excluded and do not feel intrinsically or extrinsically valued, and low retention rates for minorities. The workplace barriers that exclude minorities do not contribute to equitable conditions, productivity, creativity, and authenticity.

Leaders need to be Refractive Thinkers and embrace new and innovative approaches to DE&I. This approach requires an agile, adaptable, and open-minded leadership style. Organizational leaders must be intentional and equitable regarding how people are treated and valued in the workplace. The approach allows for an induced fit as multiple cultures and ethnic groups converge and intersect to meet organizational goals. Targeted education and strategic action create the forum for pervasive change across systems and institutions. It is time for leaders in organizations to step into a new dimension to facilitate meaningful change in DE&I.

## THOUGHTS FROM THE ACADEMIC ENTREPRENEUR

*The Problems to be Solved:*

- Understanding the interdependency of institutions in solving the Diversity, Equity, and Inclusion (DE&I) phenomenon.
- Recognizing how the Criminal Justice System as an institution contributes to the conundrum of DE&I.
- Showing how leaders in institutions can work together to affect positive change in DE&I.

*The Goals:*

- Understanding that institutions do not operate in a vacuum; behaviors in one institution can influence behaviors in another.
- Helping leaders in organizations understand that they can affect positive change in DE&I.
- Understanding how the Criminal Justice System can influence the behaviors of other institutions within America as it relates to DE&I.

*The Questions to Ask:*

- How can leaders reverse the effects of the exclusion of minorities in institutions? Can the Criminal Justice System be the driving force behind making a significant change in how minorities are viewed in American institutions?
- Can leadership in the Criminal Justice System change the culture and policies that can reverberate to other institutions to create positive opportunities for DE&I?

*Today's Business Application:*

- Leverage scholarly resources and research to prepare leaders to advocate for DE&I, create better work environments, and lead their diverse teams.

# REFERENCES

American Bar Association (ABA). (2022). *ABA profile of the legal profession.* https://www.abalegalprofile.com/

Baldwin, J. (2007). *No name in the street.* Vintage. https://www.penguinrandomhouse.com/books/7748/no-name-in-the-street-by-james-baldwin/

Baum, B. (2021). Diversity, equity, and inclusion policies: Are organizations truly committed to a workplace culture shift? *Journal of Business and Behavioral Sciences, 33*(2), 11-23. https://asbbs.org/files/2021-22/JBBS_33.2_Fall_2021.pdf

Berbeco, P. S. (2022). Authenticity at work: Global conflict with supervisors, sexual orientation, and gender identity. In C. Lentz (Ed.), *The refractive thinker®: Leading global conflict* (pp. 90-108). The Refractive Thinker® Press. https://refractivethinker.com/

Berbeco, P. S., Blowers, J., Gioia, J. A., & Epstein, M. (2022). Influence of all sexual orientations and gender identity upon work authenticity through satisfaction with supervisor. *Westcliff Journal of Applied Research, 6*(1), 6-25. https://doi.org/10.47670/wuwijar2022bbge

Bernstein, R. S., Bulger, M., Salipante, P., & Weisinger, J. Y. (2020). From diversity to inclusion to equity: A theory of generative interactions. *Journal of Business Ethics, 167*(3), 395-410. https://doi.org/10.1007/s10551-019-04180-1

Borell, B., Moewaka Barnes, H., & McCreanor, T. (2018). Conceptualizing historical privilege: The flipside of historical trauma, a brief examination. *AlterNative: An International Journal of Indigenous Peoples, 14*(1), 25-34. https://doi.org/10.1177/1177180117742202

Bourke, J., & Titus, A. (2019). Why inclusive leaders are good for organizations, and how to become one. *Harvard Business Review.* https://hbr.org/2019/03/why-inclusive-leaders-are-good-for-organizations-and-how-to-become-one

Cherry, K. (2021, March 19). *How Maslow's famous hierarchy of needs explains human motivation.* Verywell mind. https://www.verywellmind.com/what-is-maslows-hierarchy-of-needs-4136760

Darby, V., & Morrell, D. (2019). *Generations at work: A review of generational traits and motivational practices impacting millennial employees.* Semantic Scholar. https://www.semanticscholar.org/paper/Generations-at-Work%3A-A-Review-of-Generational-and-Darby-Morrell/15dbcde95edc4eb679f324dff3758fe2e-a325cb7

Dawson, M. (2018). Treating LGBTQIA patients. *Contemporary OB / GYN, 63*(12), 45-46, 48. https://www.contemporaryobgyn.net/journals/contemporary-obgyn-journal

Delaney, M., & Royal, M. (2017). Breaking engagement apart: The role of intrinsic and extrinsic motivation in engagement strategies. *Industrial and Organizational*

*Psychology, 10*(1),127-140. Breaking Engagement Apart: The Role of Intrinsic and Extrinsic Motivation in Engagement Strategies | Industrial and Organizational Psychology | Cambridge Core

Deloitte. (2021). *Diversity, equity and inclusion (DEI) transparency report.* https://www2.deloitte.com/content/dam/Deloitte/us/Documents/about-deloitte/dei-transparency-report.pdf

Fletcher, L., & Everly, B. A. (2021). Perceived lesbian, gay, bisexual, and transgender (LGBT) supportive practices and the life satisfaction of LGBT employees: The roles of disclosure, authenticity at work, and identity centrality. *Journal of Occupational & Organizational Psychology, 94*(3), 485-508. https://doi.org/10.1111/joop.12336

Francis, A. A. (2022a). *Diversity, equity, and inclusion: Organizational people leaders affecting change* (Order No. 29319285). (Doctoral dissertation, Touro University Worldwide). ProQuest One Academic. https://www.proquest.com/docview/2697162060?pq-origsite=gscholar&fromopenview=true

Francis, A. A. (2022b). Using refractive thinking to change how organizational leaders approach diversity, equity, and inclusion challenges. In C. Lentz (Ed.), *The refractive thinker®: Vol. XXII: Leading global conflict* (pp. 125-146). The Refractive Thinker® Press. https://refractivethinker.com/

Goldsen, K. F., Jen, S., Clark, T., Kim, H. J., Jung, H., & Goldsen, J. (2022). Historical and generational forces in the iridescent life course of bisexual women, men, and gender diverse older adults. *Sexualities, 25*(1-2), 132-156. https://journals.sagepub.com/home/SEX

Grissom, A. R. (2018). The alert collector: Workplace diversity and inclusion. *Reference & User Services Quarterly, 57*(4), 243. https://doi.org/10.5860/rusq.57.4.6700

Halloran, M. J. (2018). African American health and posttraumatic slave syndrome: A terror management theory account. *Journal of Black Studies, 50*(1), 45-65. https://doi.org/10.1177/0021934718803737

Haslam, S. A., Reicher, S. D., & Platow, M. J. (2020). *The new psychology of leadership: Identity, influence, and power* (2nd ed.). Routledge. https://doi.org/10.4324/9781351108232

Ifekwunigwe, J. O., Wagner, J. K., Yu, J. H., Harrell, T. M., Bamshad, M. J., & Royal, C. D. (2017). A qualitative analysis of how anthropologists interpret the race construct. *American Anthropologist, 119*(3), 422-434. https://doi.org/10.1111/aman.12890

Johnson, J. L., Adkins, D., & Chauvin, S. (2020). A review of the quality indicators of rigor in qualitative research. *American Journal of Pharmaceutical Education, 84*(1), 138-146. https://doi.org/10.5688/ajpe7120

Kossek, E. E., & Buzzanell, P. M. (2018). Women's career equality and leadership in organizations: Creating an evidence-based positive change. *Human Resource Management, 57*(4), 813-822. https://doi.org/10.1002/hrm.21936

Lambert, J. (2016). Cultural diversity as a mechanism for innovation: Workplace diversity and the absorptive capacity framework. *Academy of Educational Leadership Journal, 20*(1), 68-77. https://twu-ir.tdl.org/handle/11274/12976

Lang, K., & Spitzer, A. K. L. (2020). How discrimination and bias shape outcomes. *The Future of Children, 30*(2020), 165-186. https://doi.org/10.1353/foc.2020.0007

Maslow, A. H. (1971). *The farther reaches of human nature*. Viking. https://www.penguinrandomhouse.com/books/322518/the-farther-reaches-of-human-nature-by-abraham-h-maslow/

McKay, C. (2022). Preface. In C. Lentz (Ed.), *The refractive thinker®: Leading global conflict* (pp. 90-108). Refractive Thinker® Press. https://refractivethinker.com/

McNulty, Y., McPhail, R., Inversi, C., Dundon, T., & Nechanska, E. (2018). Employee voice mechanisms for lesbian, gay, bisexual and transgender expatriation: The role of employee-resource groups (ERGs) and allies. *International Journal of Human Resource Management, 29*(5), 829-856. https://doi.org/10.1080/09585192.2017.1376221

Miller, S. S., O'Dea, C. J., & Saucier, D. A. (2021). "I can't breathe": Lay conceptualizations of racism predict support for Black Lives Matter. *Personality and Individual Differences, 173*, 110625. https://doi.org/10.1016/j.paid.2020.110625

Pichler, S., Ruggs, E., & Trau, R. (2017). Worker outcomes of LGBT-supportive policies: A cross-level model. *Equality, Diversity and Inclusion: An International Journal, 36*(1), 17-32. https://doi.org/10.1108/EDI-07-2016-0058

Rezal, A. (2021, October 13). The racial makeup of America's prisons. *U.S. News and World Report*. https://www.usnews.com/news/best-states/articles/2021-10-13/report-highlights-staggering-racial-disparities-in-us-incarceration-rates

Rigby, C. S., & Ryan, R. M. (2018). Self-determination theory in human resource development: New directions and practical considerations. *Advances in Developing Human Resources, 20*(2), 133-147. Self-Determination Theory in Human Resource Development: New Directions and Practical Considerations - C. Scott Rigby, Richard M. Ryan, 2018 (sagepub.com)

Scott, R. C. (2021). Opening statement of chairman Robert C. "Bobby: Scott (VA-03). *Minnesota Journal of Law & Inequality, 39*(1), 5-12. https://doi.org/10.24926/25730037.620

Sharma, A., Panicker, A., & Goswami, S. (2020). Managing workplace diversity through motivation and leadership. *Paideuma Journal, 8*(3), 85-91. https://paideumajournal.com/index.php/vol-13-issue-3-march-2020/

Smedley, A. (2007). *The history of the idea of race and why it matters*. The American Anthropological Association. https://understandingrace.org/resources/research-papers/

Soni, B., & Soni, R. (2016). Enhancing Maslow's hierarchy of needs for effective leadership. *Competition Forum, 14*(2), 259-263. https://competition-forum.com/

Stewart, C., Nodoushani, O., & Stumpf, J. (2018). Cultivating employees using Maslow's hierarchy of needs. *Competition Forum, 16*(2), 67-75. https://competition-forum.com/

Tan, T. Q. (2019). Principles of inclusion, diversity, access, and equity. *The Journal of Infectious Diseases, 220*(Supplement 2), S30-S32. https://doi.org/10.1093/infdis/jiz198

Taylor, C. (2020). Diversity and inclusion. *Parks Stewardship Forum, 36*(3), 430-436. http://dx.doi.org/10.5070/P536349850

The National Association for the Advancement of Colored People (NAACP). (2023). *Criminal justice fact sheet.*. https://naacp.org/resources/criminal-justice-fact-sheet

Thoroughgood, C. N., Sawyer, K. B., Padilla, A., & Lunsford, L. (2018). Destructive leadership: A critique of leader-centric perspectives and toward a more holistic definition: JBE. *Journal of Business Ethics, 151*(3), 627-649. http://dx.doi.org/10.1007/s10551-016-3257-9

Waite, R., & Nardi, D. (2021). Understanding racism as a historical trauma that remains today: Implications for the nursing profession. *Creative Nursing, 27*(1), 19-24. https://doi.org/10.1891/CRNR-D-20-00067

Williams, R., & Smedley, A. (1994). Race in north America: Origin and evolution of a worldview. *Contemporary Sociology, 23*(3), 365-366. https://doi.org/10.2307/2075312

Williams-Washington, K. N., & Mills, C. P. (2018). African American historical trauma: Creating an inclusive measure. *Journal of Multicultural Counseling and Development, 46*(4), 246-263. https://doi.org/10.1002/jmcd.12113

Zia, S., Tabassum, N., & Noor, M. H. (2020). Analysis of gender discriminatory practices on employee motivation at the workplace: An explanatory study. *Global Management Journal for Academic & Corporate Studies, 10*(1), 87-93. https://www.gmjacs.bahria.edu.pk/index.php/ojs/article/view/138

## About the Authors...

**Dr. Anita A. Francis** was born on the island of Barbados. She is married with two sons. She currently resides in Long Island, New York. Dr. Francis has over 21 years of leadership experience leading and managing diverse and remote teams. Her research specialty is Diversity, Equity, and Inclusion in organizations, with a focus on evaluating the performance of People Leaders. She is also versed in organizational project management and strategy. Her academic and career background is in Legal Studies, Business Law, and Business Management. Dr. Francis has a Doctoral Degree in Organizational Psychology, Organizational Development, and Leadership from Touro University Worldwide.

To reach **Dr. Anita A. Francis** for information on collaborative opportunities and guest speaking, please email: Dr.AnitaAFrancis@gmail.com

**Dr. Paula Schuh Berbeco** resides with her husband of 30 years, Bob, and beloved cats in Indianapolis, Indiana. Dr. Paula has over 25 years of healthcare leadership experience in the provider and payer space. Her specialty is as an innovation advocate and change agent passionate about improving services or processes that create proven results with lasting impact. Her experience successfully leading multiple IT and business complex and simultaneous strategic programs for local, regional, and national efforts have contributed to her understanding of the challenges and opportunities facing the different levels of workers in organizations today. Her academic background includes multiple degrees and certifications in business and psychology. Dr. Paula received her doctorate in Psychology, Organizational Development, and Leadership at Touro University Worldwide. Her most recently completed research supports authenticity, diversity, and inclusion in the workplace.

To reach **Dr. Paula Schuh Berbeco** for information on collaborative opportunities, guest speaking, and consulting, please contact her through **e-mail:** DrPaulaBerbeco@gmail.com or her website https://www.DrPaulaSchuhBerbeco.com

CHAPTER 6

# A Solution to the Labor Shortage: Reformed Offenders Could be the Answer

*Dr. Karen Balcanoff, Dr. Judie Brill, Dr. Wendy J. Mizerek-Herrburger & Dr. James Wright*

Finding and retaining workers remains challenging for businesses since 2022, when the United States experienced the "Great Resignation" (U.S. Bureau of Labor Statistics, 2022a). A record number of workers, approximately 50.5 million people, quit their job in 2022 (U.S. Bureau of Labor Statistics, 2022b). The 2022 labor shortage is the result of C**** and a poor work ethic (Freeman, 2021). Unskilled and low-skilled workers are hired, not recruited, so an adjustment to hiring practices may be required (Freeman, 2021). The demand for middle-skilled workers (those with more than a high school diploma but less than a bachelor's degree) is growing, creating an opportunity for low-skilled workers if an employer will invest in up-skilling their workforce (Robinson, 2019). The opportunity to improve skills and increase financial rewards while working exists for low-skilled and skilled segments of the workforce as the labor shortage extends for an undetermined amount of time (Freeman, 2021).

Using a Refractive Thinker approach, we focused on using reformed offenders to fill the labor shortage gap. Reformed offenders should be considered in the current labor pool. With education, community biases and stereotypes toward reformed offenders can be eliminated, and by using a Refractive Thinker approach, community leaders can encourage businesses to hire these individuals. Reformation of offenders versus punitive incarceration is the goal of the correctional system (Khasni et al., 2023). Inmates are vulnerable and require additional protection for research (National Institute of Justice, 2012). We did not conduct research with live participants; we considered reformed offenders as a group of potential workers.

## Correctional Institutes' Reformation Programs

In 2020, the cost per prisoner ranged from $18,000 per year in Mississippi to $135,978 per year in Wyoming, with a state average of $45,771 (USAFacts, 2022). According to the RAND Corporation (2013), the cost of education programs in correctional institutions is $1,400 to $1,744 per participant. The average savings per participant from reduced reincarceration rates is $8,700 to $9,700 over 3 years (RAND Corporation, 2013). To reduce recidivism and save the state's taxpayer money, we explored employment opportunities for reformed offenders and whether they will sustain employment and reduce recidivism. According to McNeeley (2023), there are educational programs available for inmates that offer vocational support, employment skill enhancement, work-study programs, and social skill development, which prepare them for employment. Vocational training during incarceration can provide distraction from boredom for inmates and an opportunity for employment when reentering society (McNeill, 2022).

Dollar (2023) indicated that most correctional institutions provide educational opportunities for inmates to assist in successful transformation into society. The programs include culinary training, metalworking, sign building for our nation's interstates, barbering and cosmetology, general education opportunities to receive a high school diploma, and construction opportunities (Ciptono et al., 2023). Inmates can find guidance and support for long-term employment by participating in educational programs offered in correctional institutions (Gallant et al., 2015). One problem is reformed offenders cannot obtain occupational licenses, even if they learn the trade while in a correctional institute (Decker, 2021).

Employers indicated a unique characteristic of reformed offenders is living in an institutional lifestyle (Key & May, 2019). Reformed offenders are accustomed to being segregated from others because of their felony convictions and gender (Key & May, 2019). Working consistently after release from a correctional facility will ease the pressure of adjusting to reengagement in society by providing structure. Employers struggling to retain unskilled or low-skilled workers will work with reformed offenders (Doyle et al., 2022). There should be an evaluation processes for inmates who complete educational programs to protect businesses that hire them.

Additional challenges for reformed offenders are age, poverty, mental illnesses, education, and family status (Bushway et al., 2022). In many of our nation's correctional institutions, programs are offered to assist with mental health outreach, social services, vocational rehab, and enhanced educational opportunities to assist reformed offenders in their transition back into the communities (Austin et al., 2013). Researchers indicated that inmates who completed educational and training opportunities while incarcerated had lower recidivism rates (McNeeley, 2023). According to Bellamy et al. (2019), people with mental illness returned to prison 358 days sooner than those without a mental illness (385 days vs 743 days). The use of peer supporters (those with experience of incarceration) in community settings reduced recidivism and other health factors (Bellamy et al., 2019).

Research indicated that 68% of inmates are high school dropouts (Fight Crime: Invest in Kids, 2008), and 50% are functionally illiterate (Holzer et al., 2003). Reformed offenders lack basic education, vocational skills, and soft skills (Freise et al., 2020). Without basic skills, reformed offenders will have difficulty finding employment upon release. Soft skills are important in any job and include communication, listening, empathy, and decision-making skills. If an employee has technical skills but cannot communicate, work on a team, or is not punctual, they will not be successful in that job (Matteson et al., 2016).

In 1994, the federal government terminated Pell grants to offenders (Cantora et al., 2020). Research since 1994 showed reduced recidivism for reformed offenders who participated in correctional institute educational programs (Cantora et al., 2020). In 2015, the Department of Education began the Second Chance Pell Experimental Sites Initiative, which is a program for colleges and universities that have a partnership with a correctional institute. The financial aid for student participation in an approved program was granted, and these students can continue to apply for financial aid once released from the correctional institute. Cantora et al. (2020) indicated the students who are in correctional institutions had improved self-esteem and are motivated to continue their college classes after their release. The educational programs make the correctional institute environment safer and save each state money by reducing recidivism (Cantora et al., 2020).

Education programs need to reduce the 3-year incarceration rate by 2.6% to be cost effective. If 3% of reformed offenders do not commit a new offense 3 years following their release, the cost in education in correctional institutions has paid off (Evans et al., 2017). The cost of training and education in the correctional institute may not have a return of investment if companies will not hire graduates after their release (Graffam et al., 2004).

## Reintegrating Reformed Offenders Into Society

There is limited research about whether reformed offenders are prepared for a productive life and can achieve successful employment in their communities (Cherney, 2021). Reformed offenders need to change their mindset toward contributing to society and wanting to lead productive lives, so they can maintain employment (Cherney, 2021). If the reentry process includes supervision by a probation officer, labor opportunities may provide stabilization for the individual (Frase, 2019). Evidence supported that longer supervision by a probation officer increases the likelihood that individuals will violate their terms of release (Frase, 2019).

The U.S. Equal Employment Opportunity Commission (EEOC) (as cited in Mikkelson & Schweitzer, 2019) does not protect reformed offenders from employment discrimination because anyone convicted of a crime is not considered a vulnerable population. A criminal record discloses all illegal activity but not always the severity of the offense. A person may be arrested for shoplifting and sentenced to 2 months of probation. They did not spend time in a correctional institute but have a criminal record like a felon (Ricciardelli & Tooney, 2018). Leasure and Kaminski (2021) found more than 80% of surveyed organizations conducted criminal background checks on some job candidates, and over 60% reported conducting criminal background checks on all job candidates. According to Holloway and Wiener (2020), 68% of restaurants managers do not ask about a criminal offense but do ask about felonies. Industries, including retail, warehouse, and hospitality, were over 80% likely to check for a criminal record (Holloway & Wiener, 2020). Only nine states prohibit juvenile records from being accessed. Juvenile reformed offenders in the remaining states will have difficulty obtaining employment because employers can access their criminal records but often cannot verify if the offense occurred as a juvenile or adult (Wray, 2022). An evaluation of criminal history reporting would eliminate ambiguity and the reformed offender will have a fair chance for employment.

Public hostility exists toward reformed offenders, and they are mistreated by "invisible punishments" including not hiring them and denying them housing (Obatusin & Ritter-Williams, 2019). Reformed offenders reenter society with concerns of being discriminated against because of their criminal record and worry about receiving a fair chance, and they believe their support group, friends, and family, view them as a failure (Evans et al., 2017; Moore & Tagney, 2017). In addition to the stigma of a criminal record, reformed offenders face other stigmas, including substance abuse, race, lack of education, and mental disorders (LeBel, 2012). Social withdrawal is a coping mechanism by which reformed offenders avoid situations involving discrimination (Moore & Tagney, 2017). Self-perceived stigma causes social withdrawal, which negatively affects the reformed offenders' ability to find employment and may lead to recidivism (Moore & Tagney, 2017).

Evans et al. (2017) found inmates gained confidence when they continued their education while in a correctional institute, had less shame while completing their term, and focusing on school kept them out of trouble in the correctional institute. Upon release from the correctional institute, the reformed offenders had confidence to participate in social circles not available to them before their sentence. Respondents from Evans et al.'s study indicated the reformed offenders' friends and family were impressed they completed college degrees in a correctional institute and believed education reduced the stigma perception of their criminal record. The investment in education yields effective dividends.

The U.S. Department of Labor (DOL) Workforce Innovation and Opportunity Act of 2014 (WIOA) authorized the Reentry Employment Opportunities (REO) program designed to inform the public workforce system on how to assist reformed offenders. REO annually allocates monetary grants to community, faith-based organizations, and government systems to assist in reintegrating these individuals into the workforce (The U.S. Department of Labor [DOL], 2023). The REO program provides core services, including apprenticeships, career counseling, high school equivalency training, job placement, legal assistance, mentoring, and in-demand occupational training (DOL, 2023).

According to Obatusin and Ritter-Williams (2019), increased recidivism is caused when reformed offenders cannot find housing, employment, or a support system. Reformed offenders are easily discouraged and will become depressed and angry, resorting to illicit activities to survive (Formon et al., 2018). Reformed offenders have little to no access to U.S. federal benefits including food stamps, social security income, public housing, and student loans (Martin et. al., 2020). For a reformed offender reentering society, the lack of these benefits can result in recidivism. Black, non-Latino males are six times more likely to be imprisoned than White, non-Latino males (LeBel, 2012). Reformed offenders' race affects their ability to find a job, equally as difficult as having a criminal record (LeBel, 2012).

## Barriers to Employability

Employers are hesitant to hire reformed offenders because there is a possibility of committing workplace violence (Williams, 2007), but no empirical evidence exists linking reformed offenders and increased violence in the workplace (Mosley, 2019). Prior to release from a correctional institution, reformed offenders should receive psychological, job skills, and substance abuse rehabilitation. Before incarceration, reformed offenders had low employment rates or little job experience, mental health problems, poor health, and victimization or trauma and it is unlikely these issues were addressed while in a correctional institute, resulting in the same or worsened issues with the reformed offender (Freise et al., 2020). Reformed offenders need help after leaving a correctional institute, including financial, mental health, and substance abuse assistance. Employment is important because it gives the reformed offender an income, a role in society that will promote self-confidence, and a structured lifestyle (Heydon & Naylor, 2018; Leasure & Kaminski, 2021).

When applying for jobs, reformed offenders will be questioned about their length of time incarcerated and the nature of the offense, which will influence employability (Beasley & Xiao, 2023). Hiring managers value interviewee's disclosure of criminal convictions (Corde, 2021) and the interviewee's response and openness about their incarceration indicates honesty and that the individual believes they are an asset to the company (Wells, 2014). State-by-state restrictions determine if a reformed offender can work based on their crime (Mikkelson & Schweitzerm, 2019). Work restrictions placed by the legal system will provide insight into the employability of a reformed offender. The labor shortage continues to restrict employers' ability to meet customer needs and will require employers to create recruiting strategies and implement them (Freeman, 2021).

In 2021, the Fair Chance Act went into effect and 37 states and over 150 cities and counties have passed ordinances for fair hiring programs (National Employment Law Project, 2021). In December 2022, Gainesville, Florida, was the first city in Florida to pass a law preventing employers with 15 or more employees from rejecting job applicants because they have a criminal record (Harris, 2022). Fair hiring programs are in place to protect reformed offenders and ensure they are evaluated based on their qualifications and not their criminal history. The Fair Chance Act gives businesses a larger pool of applicants by not screening out reformed offenders.

Employers who are willing to hire reformed offenders indicated the individuals still need to go through the hiring process including applying and interviewing (Mikkelson & Schweitzer, 2019). Because they do not have soft skills, reformed offenders may have difficulty completing an application and creating a resume (Freise et al., 2020). If they have family support, the reformed offenders will have help completing the application. Being incarcerated negatively affects a reformed offender's ability to trust and engage, and they lack self-confidence (Freise et al., 2020). A lack of self-confidence will negatively affect their ability to perform well in an interview (Graffam et al., 2004). Another reason managers will not hire a reformed offender is the employee cannot be trusted because they have previously broken the law (Obatusin & Ritter-Williams, 2019). Hiring reformed offenders can negatively affect the company's reputation and success (Holloway & Wiener, 2020). The customer's perception is they do not want to conduct business with a company who will hire reformed offenders and they are a cost to the business (Obatusin & Ritter-Williams, 2019). Obatusin and Ritter-Williams (2019) interviewed a company owner who indicated they make the reformed offender employees hide when customers come in.

## Company Benefits for Hiring Reformed Offenders

Employers who hire reformed offenders give the individuals a second chance, and they want to give back to the community (Goodstein & Petrich, 2019). Employers may have been incarcerated themselves and want to "pay it forward." Motivation for hiring reformed offenders is the need for people to work laborious jobs with low skill levels like construction. These jobs are historically lower paid jobs with high turnover (Goodstein & Petrich, 2019).

Government benefits are available for managers who hire reformed offenders. The companies are eligible for UNICOR

Federal Bonding Program, which provides free theft insurance for 6 months, covering up to $5,000 per reformed offender (Federal Bureau of Prisons, n.d.). The U.S. Department of Labor has a Federal Bonding Program that protects employers from employee dishonesty, covering theft, forgery, larceny, and embezzlement (Federal Bureau of Prisons, n.d.). Companies that hire reformed offenders are eligible for the Work Opportunity Tax Credit. The IRS allows employers to claim a tax credit of up to 25% of the employee's first year's salary if they worked at least 120 hours, and 40% (maximum $6,000) of salary if they work for over 400 hours (Federal Bureau of Prisons, n.d.).

## Conclusion

In 2023, the United States continues to experience a labor shortage, especially in the areas of durable goods manufacturing, wholesale and retail trade, education, and health services (Ferguson, 2023). Workers are finding high-paying jobs remotely, alleviating the need for childcare, traveling time, gas costs, and food costs (Ferguson, 2023). Employers need to offer benefits and incentives to maintain their experienced workforce. Taking a refractive thinker approach, we researched solutions to the job shortage by using the largely untapped population of reformed offenders.

One possible answer to the labor shortage is an approach to incarceration based on rehabilitation. Providing vocational training to incarcerated individuals creates a workforce, and relocating or building factories near prisons provides job opportunities to inmates. Vocational training can be successful even with literacy challenges. This type of training is occupation-specific, giving the employer the ability to create job-specific training. Inmates can work throughout their incarceration, developing their skills, receiving acceptable wages, and be prepared for employment after release. Industry leaders create vocational training for qualifying reformed offenders that leads to an acceptable wage and quality of life.

Reformed offenders who obtain a skill during incarceration can remove themselves from the no-skill labor group (Sheppard & Ricciardelli, 2020). Finding work without skills limits the individual to manual labor with low wages and expectations (Sheppard & Ricciardelli, 2020). Working manual labor can result in low job satisfaction and wages, and therefore, substandard living. Reentering society with a marketable skill gives the reformed offender more opportunities for employment and reduces recidivism (Sheppard & Ricciardelli, 2020).

Research about the effect of incarceration on family and community indicated that sentencing length and punitive goals of incarceration can increase recidivism (Cotter, 2020). Moving reformed offenders from the no-skill labor group to low-skill or skilled groups could be an answer to the labor shortage (Freeman, 2021; Robinson, 2019). Additional research should be conducted with industries that can provide training and employment for reformed offenders that encourages them to remain in society.

## THOUGHTS FROM THE ACADEMIC ENTREPRENEUR

*The Problem to be Solved:*
- Fill the labor shortage gap
- Recidivism

*The Goals:*
- Ensure reformed offenders find employment once released from prison, which reduces recidivism.
- Provide employers a solution to the labor shortage.

*The Questions to Ask:*
- Are reformed offenders completing educational or vocational programs during incarceration?
- Can reformed offenders overcome the stigma associated with incarceration?
- Do reformed offenders receive the skills needed while incarcerated to meet the labor shortage gap when released?

*Today's Business Application:*
- Labor shortage continues to restrict employers' ability to hire workers.
- Reformed offenders can meet the business's needs with low wage expectations.

# REFERENCES

Austin, J., Cadora, E., Clear, T. R., Dansky, K., Greene, J., Gupta, V., & Young, M. C. (2013). *Ending mass incarceration: Charting a new justice reinvestment.* U.S. Department of Justice, Office of Justice Programs. https://www.ojp.gov/ncjrs/virtual-library/abstracts/ending-mass-incarceration-charting-new-justice-reinvestment

Beasley, C. R., & Xiao, Y. J. (2023) Incarceration history and ethnic bias in hiring perceptions: An experimental test of intersectional bias & psychological mechanisms. *PLoS ONE, 18*(1), 1-13. https://doi.org/10.1371/journal.pone.0280397

Bellamy, C., Kimmel, J., Costa, M. N., Tsai, J., Nulton, L., Nulton, E., Kimmel, A., Aguilar, N. J., Clayton, A., & O'Connell, M. (2019). Peer support on the "inside and outside": Building lives and reducing recidivism for people with mental illness returning from jail. *Journal of Public Mental Health, 18*(3), 188-198. https://doi.org/10.1108/JPMH-02-2019-0028

Bushway, S., Cabreros, I., Paige, J. W., Schwam, D., & Wenger, J. B. (2022). Barred from employment: More than half of unemployed men in their 30s had a criminal history of arrest. *Science Advances, 8*(7), 1-10. https://doi.org/10.1126/sciadv.abj6992

Cantora, A., Miller, J., & White, K. (2020). Implementing Pell: Challenges and successes of implementing the U.S. Department of Education's second chance Pell experimental sites initiative. *The Journal of Correctional Education, 71*(1), 2-17. https://www.jstor.org/journal/jcorreduc

Cherney, A. (2021) The release and community supervision of radicalized offenders: Issues and challenges that can influence reintegration. *Terrorism and Political Violence, 33*(1), 119-137. https://doi.org/10.1080/09546553.2018.1530661

Ciptono, W. S., Anggadwita, G., & Indarti, N. (2023). Examining prison entrepreneurship programs, self-efficacy and entrepreneurial resilience as drivers for prisoners' entrepreneurial intentions. *International Journal of Entrepreneurial Behavior & Research, 29*(2), 408-432. https://doi.org/10.1108/IJEBR-06-2022-0550

Corde, B. (2021). *Engaging an unseen workforce: Perceived hiring manager barriers when employing returning citizens* (Publication No. 28412017) [Doctoral dissertation, Northern Kentucky University]. https://www.proquest.com/openview/beed882fcb8f3917be7dcee7d84f98df/1?pq-origsite=gscholar&cbl=18750&diss=y

Cotter, R. (2020). *Length of incarceration and recidivism.* U.S. Sentencing Commission. https://www.ussc.gov/sites/default/files/pdf/research-and-publications/research-publications/2020/20200429_Recidivism-SentLength.pdf

Decker, G. (2021). Occupational licensing as a barrier for people with criminal records: Proposals to improve anti-discrimination law to address adverse employment impacts from the criminal legal system. *Urban Law Journal, 49*(1), 189-220. https://ir.lawnet.fordham.edu/ulj/vol49/iss1/6

Dollar, C. W. (2023). A new coat of paint: The bluewashing of justice reinvestment and realignment to community reinvestment. *Sociology Compass, 7*(3), 1-14. https://doi.org/10.1111/soc4.13072

Doyle, C., Yates, S., Bartels, L., Hopkins, A., & Taylor, H. (2022). 'If I don't get a job in six months' time, I can see myself being back in there': Post-prison employment experiences of people in Canberra. *Australian Journal of Social Issues, 57*(3), 627-643. https://doi.org/10.1002/ajs4.197

Evans, D. N., Pelletier, E., & Szkola, J. (2017). Education in prison and the self-stigma: Empowerment continuum. *Crime & Delinquency, 64*(2), 255-280. https://doi.org/10.1177/0011128717714973

Federal Bureau of Prisons. (n.d.). *Employing former inmates.* https://www.bop.gov/business/employing_former_inmates.jsp

Ferguson, S. (2023). *Understanding America's labor shortage: The most impacted industries.* U.S. Chamber of Commerce. https://www.uschamber.com/workforce/understanding-americas-labor-shortage-the-most-impacted-industries

Fight Crime: Invest in Kids. (2008). *School or the streets. Crime and America's dropout crisis.* https://alabamapartnershipforchildren.org/wp-content/uploads/2016/12/School-or-the-Streets-Crime-and-Americas-Dropout-Crisis.pdf

Formon, D. L., Schmidt, A. T., & Henderson, C. (2018). Examining employment outcomes of offender and nonoffender vocational program graduates. *International Journal of Offender Therapy and Comparative Criminology, 62*(9), 2781-2800. https://doi.org/10.1177/0306624X17735041

Frase, R. S. (2019). Suspended sentences and freestanding probation orders in U.S. guidelines systems: A survey and assessment. *Law and Contemporary Problems, 82*(51), 51-79. https://lcp.law.duke.edu/

Freeman, T. (2021). No easy solutions to the U.S. labor shortage. *Medical Product Outsourcing, 19*(8), 2228. https://www.mpo-mag.com/

Friese, B., Ochoa, A., Garcia, E., Hildebrandt, J., & Holmes, C. (2020). Supervising employees with criminal history: An exploratory study of manager strategies and perceptions. *International Journal of Offender Therapy and Comparative Criminology, 64*(8), 880-898. https://doi.org//10.1177/0306624X20904699

Gallant, D., Sherry, E., & Nicholson, M. (2015). Recreation or rehabilitation?: Managing sport for development programs with prison populations. *Sport Management Review, 18*(1), 45-56. https://www.sciencedirect.com/science/article/abs/pii/S1441352314000631

Goodstein, J. D., & Petrich, D. M. (2019). Hiring and retaining formerly incarcerated persons: An employer-based perspective. *Journal of Offender Rehabilitation, 58*(3), 155-177. https://doi.org/10.1080/10509674.2019.1582572

Graffam, J., Shinkfield, A., Lavelle, B., & Mcpherson, W. (2004). Variables affecting successful reintegration as perceived by offenders and professionals.

*Journal of Offender Rehabilitation, 40*(1/2), 147-171. https://doi.org/10.1300/J076v40n01_08

Harris, J. L. (2022, December 15). Hiring made more equitable for those with criminal records in Gainesville. *The Gainesville Sun.* https://www.gainesville.com/story/news/local/2022/12/15/gainesville-officials-pass-fair-chance-job-applicant-law-change/69727431007/

Heydon, G., & Naylor, B. (2018). Criminal record checking and employment: The importance of policy and proximity. *Australian & New Zealand Journal of Criminology, 51*(3), 372-394. https://doi.org//10.1177/0004865817723410

Holloway, C. P., & Wiener, R. L. (2020). Criminal history, sex, and employment: Sex differences in ex-offender hiring stigma. *Analyses of Social Issues and Public Policy, 20*(1), 211-229. https://doi.org/10.1111/asap.12192

Holzer, H. J., Raphael, S., & Stoll, M. A. (2003, May 19-20). *Employment barriers facing ex-offenders (paper presentation)*, Urban Institute Reentry Roundtable, New York University School of Law. https://www.urban.org/sites/default/files/publication/59416/410855-Employment-Barriers-Facing-Ex-Offenders.PDF

Key, A., & May, M. S. (2019). When offenders dare to become scholars: Prison education as resistance, *Review of Communication, 19*(1), 1-18. https://doi.org/10.1080/15358593.2018.1555344

Khasni, F. N., Keshminder, J. S., Chuah, S. C., & Ramayah, T. (2023). A theory of planned behaviour: perspective on rehiring ex-offenders. *Management Decision, 61*(1), 313-338. https://doi.org/10.1108/MD-08-2021-1051

Leasure, L., & Kaminski, R. J. (2021). The impact of a multiple conviction record on hiring outcomes. *Crime & Delinquency, 67*(6-7), 1022-1045. https://doi.org//10.1177/0011128720973150

LeBel, T. P. (2012). "If one doesn't get you another one will": Formerly incarcerated persons' perceptions of discrimination. *The Prison Journal, 92*(1), 63-87. https://doi.org/10.1177/0032885511429243

Martin, T. E., Huffman, A., Koons-Witt, B. A., & Brame, R. (2020). Hiring people with criminal records in South Carolina: Examining businesses' hiring practices and views on incentives. *Criminal Justice Policy Review, 31*(4), 532-554. https://doi.org/10.1177/0887403419831062

Matteson, M. L., Anderson, L., & Boyden, C. (2016). "Soft skills": A phrase in search of meaning. *Libraries and the Academy, 16*(1), 71-88. https://www.press.jhu.edu/journals/portal-libraries-and-academy

McNeeley, S. (in press). The effects of vocational education on recidivism and employment among individuals released before and during the C****-19 pandemic. *International Journal of Offender Therapy and Comparative Criminology.* https://doi.org/10.1177/0306624X231159886

McNeill, K.-M. (2022). A re-education on how to work: Vocational programs in

Kingston-area prisons, 1950-1965. *Labour/Le Travail, 89,* 61-65. https://doi.org/ https://doi.org/10.52975/llt.2022v89.005

Mikkelson, S., & Schweitzer, K. (2019). Hiring the formerly incarcerated. The mediating role of morality. *Criminal Justice and Behavior, 46*(12), 1757-1774. https://doi.org/10.1177/0093854819858373

Moore, K. E., & Tangey, J. P. (2017). Managing the concealable stigma of criminal justice system involvement: A longitudinal examination of anticipated stigma, social withdrawal, and post-release adjustment. *Journal of Social Issues, 73*(2), 322-340 https://doi.org/10.1111/josi.12219

Mosely, L. (2019). *The impact of felony criminal history on the perceptions of hiring managers citizens* (Publication No. 6930) [Doctoral dissertation, Walden University]. https://scholarworks.waldenu.edu/cgi/viewcontent.cgi?article=8209&context=dissertations

National Employment Law Project. (2021). *Ensuring people with convictions have a fair chance to work.* https://www.nelp.org/campaign/ensuring-fair-chance-to-work/

National Institute of Justice. (2012). *Challenges of conducting research in prisons.* https://nij.ojp.gov/topics/articles/challenges-conducting-research-prisons

Obatusin, O., & Ritter-Williams, D. (2019). A phenomenological study of employer perspectives on hiring ex-offenders. *Cogent Social Sciences, 5*(1), 1-13. https://doi.org//10.1080/23311886.2019.1571730

RAND Corporation. (2013). *Serving time or wasting time?* https://www.rand.org/content/dam/rand/pubs/infographics/IG100/IG113/RAND_IG113.pdf

Ricciardelli, R., & Mooney, T. (2018). The decision to disclose: Employment after prison. *Journal of Offender Rehabilitation, 57*(6), 343-366. https://doi.org/10.10 80/10509674.2018.1510866

Robinson, S. (2019). Meeting in the middle: Growth in middle-skill jobs may offer new opportunities for low-skilled workers. *TD Magazine, 73*(5), 12. https://www.td.org/td-magazine

Sheppard, A., & Ricciardelli, R. (2020). Employment after prison: Navigating conditions of precarity and stigma. *European Journal of Probation, 12*(1), 34-52. https://doi.org/10.1177/2066220320908251

Solomon, A. L. (2012). *In search of a job: Criminal records as barriers to employment.* National Institute of Justice. http://www.nij.gov/journals/270/pages/criminal-records.aspx

USAFacts. (2022). *How much do states spend on prisons?* https://usafacts.org/articles/how-much-do-states-spend-on-prisons/

U.S. Bureau of Labor Statistics. (2022a). *The "great resignation" in perspective.* https://www.bls.gov/opub/mlr/2022/article/the-great-resignation-in-perspective.htm

U.S. Bureau of Labor Statistics. (2022b). *Job openings and labor turnover.* https://www.bls.gov/news.release/jolts.nr0.htm

U.S. Department of Labor (DOL). (2023). *Reentry employment opportunities.* https://www.dol.gov/agencies/eta/reentry

Wells, D. (2014, November/December). *Training and preparing inmates for post-prison employment.* Office of Justice Programs. https://www.ojp.gov/pdffiles1/nij/248574.pdf

Williams, K. A. (2007). Employing ex-offenders: Shifting the evaluation of workplace risks and opportunities from employers to corrections. *UCLA Law Review*, 521-558. https://www.uclalawreview.org/employing-ex-offenders-shifting-the-evaluation-of-workplace-risks-and-opportunities-from-employers-to-corrections/

Wray, L. (2022). "I was just a kid": Addressing the collateral consequences of a juvenile record on employment. *Touro Law Review, 38*(1), 1523-549. https://digitalcommons.tourolaw.edu/lawreview/vol38/iss1/18/

## About the Authors...

**Dr. Karen Balcanoff** resides in Jacksonville, Florida. She has a Bachelor of Science (BHA) in Health Administration from the University of North Florida; a Master of Business Administration (MBA) from the University of North Florida; and a Doctor of Business Administration (DBA) from Walden University. Dr. Karen began the first bachelor program at St. Johns River State College in January 2011 and teaches, advises, and mentors all students in the program. Prior to joining St. Johns River State College, she was an educator at Flagler Hospital in St. Augustine, Florida.

Dr. Karen co-authored "Conflict in Higher Education" in *The Refractive Thinker©*, Volume XXII; "New and Emerging Tools and Trends in Project Management" in *The Refractive Thinker©*, Volume XVIII; "Nonprofit and For-Profit Healthcare Organization Satisfaction based on Compensation Packages" in *The Refractive Thinker©*, Volume XIV; and "Doctoral Mentoring and Research Leading to Emerging Technologies" in *The Refractive Thinker©*, Volume IX. She also co-authored published articles "Engaging Employees Successful in Project Management Practices" and "Best Practices in Doctoral Retention: Mentoring." Dr. Karen gained professional and academic expertise with her doctoral study, *The Effect of Communication on Hospital Nursing and Morale*.

To reach **Dr. Karen Balcanoff** for additional information, professional editing, or guest speaking, please **e-mail:** karenbalcanoff@sjrstate.edu

**Dr. Judie L. Brill** resides in the mountain town of Bailey, Colorado. Dr. Judie holds accredited degrees a Bachelor of Science (BS) in Biological Sciences from the University of Nebraska; a Master of Arts Management (MAM) from Doane College; and a Doctor of Business Administration (DBA) from Walden University.

Dr. Judie is a consultant for the pharmaceutical industry specializing in business processes, strategies, lean leadership, and project management. She enjoys the interaction with numerous companies, employees, and regulatory agencies striving to provide a pathway to excellence within diverse organizations. She is a member of the IPSE Mountain States Chapter and other Pharmaceutical and Lean Six Sigma Organizations.

Dr. Judie is President and CEO of Brill Consulting, Inc., a Professional organizational consulting company. Her doctoral study, A *Company's Response to Culture Change in Time of Reorganization* provided her the opportunity to gain professional and academic expertise to facilitate improvements in the changing world of manufacturing and pharmaceutical industries. Dr. Judie co-authored "New and Emerging Tools and Trends in Project Management" in *The Refractive Thinker*©, Volume XVIII; "Nonprofit and For-Profit Healthcare Organization Satisfaction based on Compensation Packages" in *The Refractive Thinker*©, Volume XIV; and "Doctoral Mentoring and Research Leading to Emerging Technologies" in *The Refractive Thinker*©, Volume IX. She co-authored published articles "Engaging Employees Successful in Project Management Practices" and "Best Practices in Doctoral Retention: Mentoring."

To reach **Dr. Judie L. Brill** for information on consulting or doctoral coaching, please **e-mail:** judie.brill@gmail.com

**Dr. Wendy J. Mizerek-Herrburger** resides in the Space coast town of Cocoa Beach, Florida. Dr. Wendy holds a Bachelor of Science (BS) in Marketing from the University of Florida; a Master of Science in Industrial Engineering (MSIE) from the University of Central Florida; and a Doctor of Business Administration (DBA) in Leadership from Walden University.

Dr. Wendy is a Division Manager at the ARES Corporation at the Kennedy Space Center, Florida supporting the Exploration Ground Systems Program.

Dr. Wendy co-authored "New and Emerging Tools and Trends in Project Management" in *The Refractive Thinker*®, *Volume XVIII;* "Nonprofit and For-Profit Healthcare Organization Satisfaction based on Compensation Packages" in *The Refractive Thinker*®, *Volume XIV;* and "Doctoral Mentoring and Research Leading to Emerging Technologies" in *The Refractive Thinker*®, *Volume IX*. She also co-authored published articles "Engaging Employees Successful in Project Management Practices" and "Best Practices in Doctoral Retention: Mentoring."

To reach **Dr. Wendy J. Mizerek-Herrburger**, please **e-mail**: drwendy herrburger@outlook.com.

 **Dr. James Wright** resides in Perrysburg, Ohio. He has a Bachelor of Science in Human Resources Management (HRM) from Park University, a Master of Arts in Organizational Management (MAOM) from The University of Phoenix, and a Doctor of Business Administration (DBA) in Leadership from Walden University.

Dr Jim is a Senior Clinical Specialist working in the Behavioral Health business unit of a specialty pharmaceutical company. Prior to working in the pharmaceutical industry, he spent 20 years in the U.S. Navy. He retired as a Senior Chief. His assignments during his service included time on ships, overseas commands, and recruiting organizations.

Dr. Jim co-authored "New and Emerging Tools and Trends in Project Management" in *The Refractive Thinker©*, Volume XVIII, and "Nonprofit and For-Profit Healthcare Organization Satisfaction based on Compensation Packages" in *The Refractive Thinker©*, Volume XIV. Dr. Jim gained professional and academic expertise with his doctoral study, *Manufacturing Managers' Leadership Efficacy in the Context of Reduced Union Influence*.

To reach **Dr. James Wright** for information on business or leadership consulting, please **e-mail**: jwright2962@gmail.com

CHAPTER 7

# Educate or Litigate? The Mindsets of Advancing Knowledge and Maintaining Financial Stability in Higher Education

*Dr. Cherri Brown & Dr. Cheryl Lentz*

The educational mindset for online higher degrees, specifically the master's and doctoral journey, shifted from the refractive thinking perspective as transformational experiences, producing objective decision-making processes, to transactional business exchanges, and in some institutions, an exchange for investors and stakeholders. Nehrlich (2006) coined "transactional exchange" as an exchange of one thing for another involving some form of gain. This chapter presents the business of marketing higher education programs (i.e., master's and doctoral degrees) and the front-line faculty positioned to achieve an institution's profit margin derived from degree production. Our goal is to discuss the losses and gains when faculty, who previously focused on innovation, comparative thinking, and mentoring, add an institution's financial stability to their responsibilities (Kaufman-Osborn, 2023). Stakeholder needs range from graduating learners with innovative ideas to meeting an institution's financial needs (Ramadoss et al., 2022). While the profit margins of public institutions have dropped precipitously (Macrotrends, 2023), for-profit and not-for-profit institutions of higher education must leverage program efficacy with financial viability (Wally Boston, 2020). In the United States, private and increasingly public postsecondary institutions must consider political goals; thus, for-profit and not-for-profit institutions can experience increased demands for financial solvency. The profitability versus a learner's goals then must undergo a balancing exercise. This chapter briefly explores the progression of academic faculty from traditional harbingers of innovative programs to increased profitability, a nuanced yet pervasive mindset (PEW, 2019; Schwartz, 2022).

Academic transactional exchanges are guided by an accrediting private or public agency (i.e., state and regional agencies recognized by the U.S. Department of Education). The agencies have specific educational learning program criteria that educators and their institutions must meet in their classrooms and programs. The educator mindset exudes respect for the accreditation process, the learner, the course, and the program focus. Silver and Lentz (2012) coined the term "consumer learner" and highlighted the move from a transformational education mindset to a transactional customer service mindset. The transactional mindset continues to grow and evolve based on litigation paranoia brought on by learners as a premise of "the customer is always right" [or] "the customer is never wrong" (Morgan, 2018). That mindset emanates from a position of what we authors deem as process ownership and learner perspective outcome, the "my dollar, my choices" mindset. This chapter aims to share the importance of what we have found in master's and doctoral programs. Do we, as educators, educate or prepare for increasing litigation from learners in online and ground-based doctoral programs? A growing number of individual and class action lawsuits are part of a new perspective that affects the laws and practices from program marketing to our judicial system, such as University of Southern California, Northcentral University, Capella University, and others (U.S. Department of Education, 2023).

## The Higher Purpose of Higher Education

At its core, the American dream represents belief and trust in an individual's pursuit of "certain unalienable rights, that among these is life, liberty, and the pursuit of happiness" (Bill of Rights Institute, 2023), often found in the pursuit of higher education and how an earned degree provides principles of "unalienable rights." The American dream symbolized hope, prosperity, and happiness, believed possible via education. F. Scott Fitzgerald's *The Great Gatsby*, foretold what we witness in higher degree programs, online and ground-based (i.e., brick and mortar) institutions (Jeanpierre, 2013). Fitzgerald used his characters to express a "struggle against the identity their society" gave them (Jeanpierre, 2013, p. 1). Jeanpierre's (2013) interpretation is categorized as knowledge, mainly via postsecondary degrees, and promises of wealth, prestige, and business acumen. The inherent nature of pursuing and attaining higher academic credentials of affluence, a joy of learning, and personal success, represented an individual's choice to obtain a higher education degree (Adair, 2001).

Traditionally considered keepers of expanded knowledge, higher education professors were heralded as respected community members (Boyer, 2016). Professors understood the importance of higher education and its credentials (Chan, 2016). Professors maintain promising careers and are well regarded at the master's and doctoral level; however, up to 25% of professors surveyed in 2020 were below the income poverty line as the increase in adjunct professors heralded a way to balance costs (Herder, 2022; Inside Scholar Community, 2023). A rise in the job outlook for professors is expected (U.S. Bureau of Labor Statistics, 2023); however, increasing degree costs and decreasing state and federal funding support leaves learners obtaining funding through private sources and institutions relying on U.S. federally funded loans (Kelchin, 2019; Urban Institute, 2017), as a part of their financial stability needs. Intense marketing to attract master's and doctoral students by some institutions and increasing litigious actions by groups (i.e., class action suits from students at Tier 1-3 colleges and universities, online nonprofit and for-profit institutions, and brick-and-mortar institutions) against the institutions and their faculty occur when learners' expectations clash with accrediting agencies and doctoral program requirements (Schwartz, 2022).

From Dewey's (1897) *My Pedagogic Creed* to Seltzer-Kelly's (2008) *Deweyan Darwinism for the Twenty-First Century*, education guided by science for "democratic participation" (Seltzer-Kelly, 2008, p. 289) was the purpose of all levels of education. Ramadoss et al. (2022) posited that higher education prepared graduates for future challenges in all disciplines, focusing on the evolution of technology in all aspects of America. The authors added that higher education provides tools (i.e., internships and career guidance) to prepare and sustain students as good citizens throughout their lives (Brookfield, 1987).

## What Happened?

The traditional transformational experience and rules of the game and, we suggest, the educational mindset have accepted a transactional business exchange in the obtention of an academic certification or credential. The expectation was that a learner's degree involved an exchange of personal investment (i.e., personal resources) as a business transaction, an expectation as one might expect when purchasing a home (Silver & Lentz, 2012). What once was an exchange of financial aid and investment for the opportunity to pursue future success became an expectation of quid pro quo, a grade for a fee. With the paradigm shift from a refractive thinking perspective, transformational experience to one of transactional exchange, unintentional consequences crossed into the realm of justice where anything less than completing a transactional exchange of a fee for certification or credential was unacceptable to the learner. Final graduation and conferment of a degree defined by the authority vested in a university provost or dean expanded to litigation in civil courtrooms and the court of public opinion (McKenzie, 2017).

## The Educational Promise Moved to Chambers

Legal teams, much like "ambulance chasers," included higher education in their portfolio of clients, and we describe them as "degree chasers" (Schwartz, 2022). Since 2000, the number of class action lawsuits has increased in higher education and, more so, in doctoral than master's programs (Cappellino, 2022; Greising & Roberson, 2022). Final decisions about grade attainment have traditionally been the purview of the academic dean (Washington University in St. Louis, 2023). Despite the foundation of the American dream, higher education learners have invited judges to the classroom and academic programs for various reasons that focus on marketing promises, such as the time to complete a degree (Cappellino, 2022). Judges and juries are not faculty in higher education and are not Refractive Thinkers as educators because they are arbiters of local, state, and federal laws. However, they have become de facto members of degree determinants, an unintended consequence with far-reaching implications for higher learning institutions and the knowledge they provide for future influential leaders of the world (Greising & Roberson, 2022; Schwartz, 2022).

Faculty training includes documenting all faculty and learner communications and creating a "paper trail" to justify actions that faculty and administration may legally call upon to defend, whereas previously, training was devoted to faculty development

(Ball, 2019; McQuiggan, 2014). Faculty receive training to protect themselves and their institution first and foremost as a teaching best practice based on a foundation of what we call "eduparanoia." With every pen swipe, faculty feedback, assignments, grades, and cheating can be challenged as court cases and filings provide evidence of eduparanoia (Schwartz, 2022). Increasingly, learners submit work completed by hired editors, methodologists, and content experts as original work, despite institutional violations of student conduct regulations (du Boulay, 2023). In our opinion, the litigation mindset has a permanent home in the hallowed halls of academia.

## Faculty as Police

In institutions of higher learning, advances in artificial intelligence (AI), especially programs that can pass a law school test and author postsecondary essays (Sloan, 2023), faculty are tasked with integrity enforcement. Learners can purchase papers from various online sources (i.e., STUDYclerk and Custom Research Papers). The latest software programs do not require a third party because the programs can write a paper without detection by any leading plagiarism program (i.e., Turnitin or SafeAssign software programs).

## Build a Better Mouse Trap: Students Find a Better Mouse

In the online learner space, student surrogacy (i.e., hiring a professional in any discipline to complete course and degree requirements) learners can outsource participation in an online course, despite live online video and audio programs, the "mouse traps" for integrity (Glassman et al., 2023). The task in that situation has been up to educators to scan social media programs that match faces on a screen with faces in a learner's social media posts (i.e., LinkedIn and Facebook). Learners are acquiring an increasingly better mouse.

## The Litigation Mindset

Instead of naively believing that a faculty member's role was to impart knowledge to the next generation, the goal is now to teach with a litigation mindset. This new premise is to avoid litigation or losing a position because a paper trail via recordings and copies of digital communications may not suffice. Faculty must protect themselves from technology designed to outsmart the faculty, institution, and, as we contend, a future business owner. We authors posit that faculty has become a de facto cyber police, trained in counter-cheating best practices. Faculty must now carve out additional and often countless hours away from their dutiful and loved teaching and mentoring actions to create a digital and paper trail for each learner, including recorded meetings via such programs as SKYPE and Zoom. SKYPE and Zoom offer transcripts of recorded meetings. The digital and paper trails must be kept for sometimes years to address student accusations. The accusations amount to a disparagement of requiring integrity and original work in a classroom, regardless of location. Original work from learners represents espousing their purpose and contributing within and outside their communities.

The more nefarious goal is pursuing a personal and Machiavellian-type endeavor when an end will justify the means to a master's or terminal degree. Chan (2016) and Ramadoss et al. (2022) suggested that academic credentialing could offer a higher probability of success in screening potential candidates. We lament the advent of achieving credentials and promotion with minor investment and effort possible.

To secure employment, the graduate must confirm their credentials. Note that we **do not** include the word "learning."

While faculty must constantly search for plagiarism, cheating, and student surrogacy, online master's and doctoral learning is increasingly popular with an adult, nontraditional learner (i.e., learners aged 25 years and older) (CAEL, 2021). Moreover, while faculty have noted decreased freedom in online classrooms, Lederman (2020) noted an increasing acceptance and preference for online learning at all levels (i.e., primary grades and postsecondary degrees). Shreaves et al. (2020) found that online faculty at a "midsized liberal arts university located in the Pacific Northwest portion of the United States" (p. 110) had mixed feelings. In opposition to faculty understanding that online coursework increased knowledge with increased learners, faculty acknowledged their misgivings about a decreased flexibility when it called into question their "personal teaching values" (Shreaves et al., 2020, p. 120).

When we began teaching careers in the late 1990s, we were tasked with proof of academic credentials, often including referrals from our dean, faculty, and other employment outside of our educational employment, as proof of attainment, credibility, and trustworthiness. In the early millennium, faculty often had to submit to local, state, and federal criminal background checks, including fingerprinting and federal government clearances. While we understand the need to protect our learners, we remain concerned about the validity of those checks if and when confronted by an individual or group lawsuit about our skills or grades not earned by a learner but demanded by a learner. A faculty meeting over a decade ago led to retitling faculty as customer service agents that resulted in being "deputized" in the service of the higher education cyber policing without training. The increasingly slow erosion of the American dream and the faculty's role in pursuing that dream is not good news.

Faculty receive more scrutiny than previous generations because faculty and administration must adjudicate and investigate student complaints and are modeled best by Princeton University's procedures for all university members (Princeton University, 2023). When faculty are questioned about their personal beliefs, feelings, and thoughts as a justified accusation by a learner, abdicating the innocent until proven guilty defense, the result can be litigation. An accusation of an unfair grade needs only a verbal or written complaint to begin investigating a faculty or institution (Masis, 2007). The standard route is through the professor, department chair, dean, and sometimes a person in the institution who serves as a mediator between learner and institution.

## There is a New Sheriff in Town: Faculty Security Force, Cyber Resilience

Faculty are challenged by how to keep up with changes in technology that can increase unfair and unjust accusations that result in the unfair position of faculty as officers of a cybersecurity force, particularly among the over 50% of faculty now serving as adjuncts (Flaherty, 2022). Faculty must incorporate what the group "saltycloud" (SaltyCloud, 2023) describes as cyber resilience. The advent of what we call "adjunctery" was an original form of transitional exchange because adjuncts received few or no benefits, such as medical and, more importantly, tenure. Adjuncts were not heavily involved in or aware of the advent of AI and its venture into all levels of education. AI programs create essays and substitute for learners in online classes and test-taking (du Boulay, 2023). The policing that faculty must now do is an uncompensated task that requires additional hours from the 168 hours all humans have within a 7-day week and requires faculty to add a minimum of an hour per learner for each assignment to go through the growing new needs of traditional reading, grading, mentoring, and motivating.

## Student Faculty Relationship

The relationship between students and faculty cannot allow students to continue to use technology to cheat and still expect the sanctity of the student and professor relationship. Students sign integrity pledges with their college or university not to cheat, then cheat, and accuse faculty of wrongdoing when cheating is discovered (Borgos et al., 2023, p. 365).

## The End Game: The End of the Educational Promise?

As a result of a student's earned (or as we posit, potentially unearned) credentials, they graduate and apply for a job and the Dewey (1897) and Seltzer-Kelley (2008) promises become irrelevant. Stanny and Urbanski (2022) found that "policy actors" were, as we coin them, disruptors to the traditional mindset of educators in favor of policies that led to the litigation factor that faculty must now contend with, the eduparanoia factor. Eduparanoia is evident in the resumes and curriculum vitae of graduates who purchase a service to enhance, embellish, and sometimes lie to impress potential employers (Bixler, 2019). Bixler (2019) warned that discovering falsehoods on resumes often results in rejection. An unintended consequence is an institution's and faculty's reputation because their names on theses and dissertations (Escandon-Barbosa et al., 2023). There are human resource department (HRD) employees tasked solely with checking the credentials of institutions named in an applicant's documents submitted for employment (Brunner, n.d.). The result of an embellished, enhanced, and or falsehood by applicants is that once hired or on paid probation that leads to full employment, end in termination of employment. Businesses include a "temp-to-hire option" for candidates to demonstrate the skills listed in their application documents. The degree of falsehoods then leads to, in some cases, litigation that reflects poorly on the institution and, more often, individual faculty members.

Cheating on an employment application is not limited to alleged wasted or broken promises or dreams of what a learner expects with a master's or doctorate. Cheating also denigrates the degrees of graduates from the same institution as a cheater and who earned their credentials without cheating. Thus, the doors to our judicial system open. Apprenticeships and temp-to-hire positions have always held the promise of discovering a good fit between applicant and employer with the understanding that the applicant had well-earned employment document statements and credentials. The employer confidence is jeopardized with the advent of cheating ease and eduparanoia faculty. The outcome of a degree is to game's rules have always been to demonstrate skills. A former professor to one of us suggested that students would not want to end up on a gurney in an emergency room, wondering if the hospitalist in charge of whether we would live or die cheated on an exam. Leaving any part of our life to a cheater is not an option.

## Conclusion

The educational mindset is transforming within higher education, notably at the master's and doctoral level for learners and faculty. What was considered a transformational experience in pursuit of a degree, has evolved into a transactional business exchange. In the past, educators were responsible for their teaching skills, where educational learning outcomes were the prime focus. Instead, the educator's mindset has evolved into a litigation mindset born from apprehension and paranoia of being sued. The purpose of our chapter is to share the importance of what continues to evolve in higher education. We prefer and want to educate within a refractive thinking mindset, and not within a mindset of litigation.

## THOUGHTS FROM THE ACADEMIC ENTREPRENEUR

*The Problem to be Solved:*

- Evolution from an educational mindset to a litigation one.

*The Goals:*

- Understanding how to prepare for teaching in higher education when the focus is faculty as cyber security police.

*The Questions to Ask:*

- Educate or litigate?
- Faculty professor or customer service agent?

*Today's Business Application:*

- Recognize the evolution of the pursuit of higher education as a transformational opportunity to a transactional business exchange.
- Recognize the need of additional time spent by faculty in documentation of all aspects of the faculty and student relationship in anticipation and preparation of potential future litigation.
- Recognize the misplaced expectation that earning academic credentials displaces academic learning as priority focus.
- Recognize the influence on business owners when hiring graduates to confirm skillset demonstration indicated on employment documents.

# REFERENCES

Adair, V. (2001). Poverty and the (broken) promise of higher education. *Harvard Educational Review*, 71(2), 217-240. https://doi.org/10.17763/haer.71.2.k3gx0kx755760x50

Ball, M. (2019). *Teaching online part one: What's your liability?* Alternative Balance. https://support.alternativebalance.com/hc/en-us/articles/360051155834-Teaching-Online-Part-One-What-s-your-liability-

Bill of Rights Institute. (2023). *Declaration of independence*. https://billofrightsinstitute.org/primary-sources/declaration-of-independence?gclid=Cj0KCQjwn9CgBhDjARIsAD15h0Cy30AOt4YUJKkatexMwj4Xoo2yt-1k8XF1LlHxxYzCDsxnmIdygm3YaAuv9EALw_wcB

Bixler, R. (2019, September 24). Lying on your resume: Consider this advice before embellishing your career. *U.S. News & World Report*. https://money.usnews.com/money/blogs/outside-voices-careers/articles/lying-on-your-resume-consider-this-advice-before-embellishing-your-career

Borgos, J., Kinser, K., & Kline, L. (2023). The borderless market for open, distance, and digital education. In O. Zawacki-Richter & I. Jung (Eds.), *Handbook of open, distance and digital education* (pp. 356-368). Springer. https://doi.org/10.1007/978-981-19-2080-6

Boyer, J. W. (2016) *Academic freedom and the modern university: The experience of the University of Chicago*. https://news.uchicago.edu/sites/default/files/attachments/Academic_Freedom_V1.pdf

Brookfield, S. D. (1987). *Developing critical thinkers: Challenging adults to explore alternative ways of thinking and acting*. Jossey-Bass. https://eric.ed.gov/?id=ED294480

Brunner. (n.d.). *What does "institution" mean on a job application?* Salarship. https://salarship.com/article/institution-job-application/

CAEL. (2021). *Insights and opportunities: Student parents & behavioral science*. Cael. https://www.cael.org/hubfs/CanBehavioralScienceHelpCollegeStudentswithChildrenGraduate.pdf

Cappellino, A. (2022). *More than 70 universities sued for refunds following C\*\*\*\*-19 campus closures*. Expert Institute. https://www.expertinstitute.com/resources/insights/universities-sued-for-covid-19-refunds-following-campus-closures/

Chan, R. Y. (2016). Understanding the purpose of higher education: An analysis of the economic and social benefits for completing a college degree. *Journal of Education Policy, Planning and Administration*, 6(5), 1-41. https://scholar.harvard.edu/files/roychan/files/chan_r._y._2016._understanding_the_purpose_aim_function_of_higher_education._jeppa_65_1-40.pdf

Dewey, J. (1897). My pedagogic creed. *School Journal, 54*, 77-80. http://dewey.pragmatism.org/creed.htm

du Boulay, B. (2023). Artificial intelligence in education and ethics. In O. Zawacki-Richter & I. Jung (Eds.), *Handbook of open, distance and digital education* (pp. 93-106). Springer.

Escandon-Barbosa, D., Salas-Paramo, J., & Moreno-Gómez, J. (2023). Academic reputation quality and research: An analysis of Latin-American universities in the world higher education institution rankings from the perspective of organizational learning theory. *Journal of Further and Higher Education*. Advance online publication. https://www.tandfonline.com/doi/pdf/10.1080/0309877X.2023.2176204

Flaherty, C. (2022). *Pushed out*. Inside Higher Ed. https://www.insidehighered.com/news/2022/11/29/ut-southwestern-settles-long-running-discrimination-case

Glassman, A., Lentz, C., & Bollenback, D. (2023). Where's Waldo: IP address incongruence and student surrogacy. In V. P. Denney & C. J. Roberts (Eds.), *Building honor in academics: Case studies in academic integrity* (pp. 18-24). Jossey-Bass. https://www.wiley.com/en-us/Building+Honor+in+Academics:+Case+Studies+in+Academic+Integrity-p-9781119880547

Greising, R. A., & Roberson, E. M. (2022). *Class action against sixteen universities for alleged unlawful practices in awarding financial aid*. Krieg|Devault. https://www.kriegdevault.com/insights/class-action-against-sixteen-universities-for-alleged-unlawful-practices-in-awarding-financial-aid

Herder, L. (2022, February 24). *Adjunct faculty struggled with finances and job security during the pandemic. diverse issues in higher education*. Diverse issues in Higher Education. https://www.diverseeducation.com/latest-news/article/15288972/adjunct-faculty-struggled-with-finances-job-security-during-pandemic

Inside Scholar Community. (2023). *The rise of adjunct faculty*. https://blog.insidescholar.org/the-rise-of-adjunct-faculty/

Jeanpierre. S. (2013). *The Great Gatsby and the struggle for wealth, purity, and the pursuit of identity*. [Doctoral dissertation, California State University, Bakersfield]. Scholarworks, California State University. https://scholarworks.calstate.edu/downloads/pr76f7594

Kaufman-Osborn, T. V. (2023). *The autocratic academy: Reenvisioning rule within America's universities*. Duke University Press. https://www.dukeupress.edu/the-autocratic-academy

Kelchen, R. (2017, January 11). *How much do for-profit colleges rely on federal funds?* Brookings Institution. https://www.brookings.edu/blog/brown-center-chalkboard/2017/01/11/how-much-do-for-profit-colleges-rely-on-federal-funds/

Lederman, D. (2020, October 6). *Faculty confidence in online learning grows*. Inside Higher Ed. https://www.insidehighered.com/digital-learning/article/2020/10/06/covid-era-experience-strengthens-faculty-belief-value-online

Macrotrends. (2023). *American public education profit margin 2010-2022.* https://www.macrotrends.net/stocks/charts/APEI/american-public-education/profit-margins

Masis, J. (2007, February 7). *Student sues university over grade.* Reuters. https://www.reuters.com/article/us-student-lawsuit/student-sues-university-over-grade-idUSN0725021320070208

McKenzie, L. (2017, October 18). *Questions on quality of online learning.* Inside Higher Ed. https://www.insidehighered.com/digital-learning/article/2017/10/18/faculty-analysis-criticizes-online-education-george-washington

McQuiggan, C. A. (n.d.). Faculty development for online teaching as a catalyst for change. *Journal of Asynchronous Learning Networks, 16*(2), 27-61. https://files.eric.ed.gov/fulltext/EJ971044.pdf

Morgan, B. (2018). *A global view of 'the customer is always right.'* Forbes. https://www.forbes.com/sites/blakemorgan/2018/09/24/a-global-view-of-the-customer-is-always-right/?sh=2f3929dd236f

Nehrlich, E. (2006, November 1). *Transactional exchanges.* Unrepentant Generalist. https://www.nehrlich.com/blog/2006/11/01/transactional-exchanges/

PEW. (2019). *Two decades of change in federal and state higher education funding.* https://www.pewtrusts.org/en/research-and-analysis/issue-briefs/2019/10/two-decades-of-change-in-federal-and-state-higher-education-funding

Ramadoss. D., Bolgioni, A. F., Layton, R. L., Adler, J., Luyndsteen, N., Stayart, C. A., Yellin, J. B., Smart, C. L., & Varayanis, S. S. (2022). Using stakeholder insights to enhance engagement in PhD professional development. *Plos One, 17*(1), 1-23. https://doi.org/10.1371/journal.pone.0262191

Princeton University. (2023). *Rights, rules, responsibilities.* https://rrr.princeton.edu/2022/university-wide-regulations/17-resolution-complaints-against-members-university-community

SaltyCloud. (2023). *Citer resilience at higher education institutions: The definitive guide for information security teams.* https://www.saltycloud.com/resources/cyber-resilience-in-higher-education-guide/

Schwartz, N. (2022, January 11). *6 higher education lawsuits to watch in 2022.* Higher Ed Dive. https://www.highereddive.com/news/6-higher-education-lawsuits-to-watch-in-2022/617005/

Seltzer-Kelly, D. (2008). Deweyan Darwinism for the twenty-first century: Toward an educational method for critical democratic engagement in the era of the Institute of Education Sciences. *Educational Theory, 68*(3), 289-304. https://doi.org/10.1111/j.1741-5446.2008.00289.x

Shreaves, D. L., Ching, Y. H, Uribe-Florez, L., & Trespalacios, J. (2020). Faculty perceptions of online teaching at a midsized liberal arts university. *Online Learning, 24*(3), 106-127. https://files.eric.ed.gov/fulltext/EJ1271800.pdf

Silver, G., & Lentz, C. A. (2012). *The consumer learner: Emerging expectations of a customer service mentality in postsecondary education.* Pensiero Press. https://pensieropress.com

Sloan, K. (2023, January 25). *chatGPT passes law school exams despite 'mediocre' performance.* Reuters. https://www.reuters.com/legal/transactional/chatgpt-passes-law-school-exams-despite-mediocre-performance-2023-01-25/

Stanny, E., & Urbanski, J.C. (2022). Reducing and detecting on-line exam cheating: Building a better mousetrap protocols for Canvas and other learning management systems. *Business Education Innovation Journal, 14*(1), 98-104. http://www.beijournal.com/

Urban Institute. (n.d.). *Understanding college affordability: Borrowing.* https://collegeaffordability.urban.org/covering-expenses/borrowing/#/

U.S. Bureau of Labor Statistics. (2023). *Career outlook.* https://www.bls.gov/careeroutlook/2023/home.htm

U.S. Department of Education, Federal Student Aid. (2023, March 14). (*General-23-14) FSA enforcement bulletin, March 2023-Announcing use of secret shoppers to evaluate recruitment and enrollment practices and monitor Title IV compliance.* https://fsapartners.ed.gov/knowledge-center/library/electronic-announcements/2023-03-14/fsa-enforcement-bulletin-march-2023-announcing-use-secret-shoppers-evaluate-recruitment-and-enrollment-practices-and-monitor-title-iv-compliance

Wally Boston. (2020, May 8). *How should we measure financial solvency for colleges and universities.* https://wallyboston.com/financial-solvency-colleges-universities/

Washington University in St. Louis. (2023). *Dean roles and responsibilities.* https://research.wustl.edu/about/roles-responsibilities/dean/#:~:text=Deans%20are%20academic%20leaders%20who,%2C%20admission%2C%20and%20academic%20progress

## *About the Authors ...*

**Dr. Cherri L. Brown** is known to her learners as Dr. B, Dr. Brown, and Dr. Cherri. She is a Georgia Neutral, adjunct professor at Andrew College, and Senior Adjunct Dissertation Committee Chair with Grand Canyon University. She offers online mentoring, is a freelance writer, editor, published journal author, Mount Holyoke College Fund Raiser Program Coordinator, life coach, and editorial services for groups and individuals. Dr. Cherri served as an APA mentor for the Walden University community. Academic credentials include an associate of arts in Education and Biosciences from Miami Dade Community College (now a 4-year college); a Bachelor of Arts in Education and Psychology, with minor in Ethics, from Mount Holyoke College; and a PhD in Psychology Education from Walden University. She also has an MBA in Healthcare, HR, from NY Institute of Technology. Dr. Cherri is studying for the Georgia State therapizing license. Justice Center of Atlanta, Mediation, Betty Manley School of Mediation, Family, and a life coach certificate. Motivational Speaker.

Publications include *Does My Doctor Listen?* (in review); Food Editor, Scripts-Howard, Sun Sentinel, The San Juan Star; *Independent Living Oldest-Old and their Primary Health Provider, A Mixed-Method Examination of the Influence of Patient Personality Characteristics. Examination of the Influence Cultural Cognition for Learning English: A Mexican Immigrant Family's Perspective* (Doctoral Dissertation); *The Psychology of Language: Because* (in review), *Grandparents Parenting: Mediation Solutions, Association for Conflict Resolution; Bullying in Elementary School: Learning to Self-Modify Behavior with Peers* [unpublished]; *The Influence of Teacher as Learner on Short-and Long-Term Retention*, Mount Holyoke College Archives.

To reach **Dr. Cherri Brown** for additional information or guest speaking, please **e-mail:** clbgate@gmail.com, cbrown@neutralplace.com or doc.cherri brown@gmail.com

 **Dr. Cheryl Lentz**, affectionately known as *Doc C* to her students, is a university professor on faculty with Embry-Riddle Aeronautical University, Grand Canyon University, and Walden University. Dr. Cheryl serves as a dissertation mentor / chair and committee member. She is also a dissertation coach, offering expertise as a professional editor for APA style for graduate thesis and doctoral dissertations, as well as faculty journal publications and books.

Awards include Walden Faculty of the Year, DBA Program, UOP community service award, and 26 writing awards.

Known globally for her writings on leadership and failure, as well as critical and refractive thinking, she has been published more than 57 times to include her favorite, Best Seller: *Failure Has No Alibi*. Additional published works include her dissertation: *Strategic Decision Making in Organizational Performance,* her first children's book: *Two Babies in a Manager,* as well as *Journey Outside the Golden Palace, The Consumer Learner, Technology That Tutors, Effective Study Skills, The Dissertation Toolbox*, International Best Seller: *The Expert Success Solution,* and contributions to the award winning series: *The Refractive Thinker®: Anthology of Doctoral Learners, Volumes I–XXIII.*

She took the stage as a **TEDx Speaker** in *Farmingdale2020, October 10, 2020. https://www.youtube.com/watch?v=PbHlUPn7arQ

To reach **Dr. Cheryl Lentz** for information on refractive thinking, professional editing, or motivational speaking, please visit her **website:** http://DrCherylLentz.com or **e-mail:** drcheryllentz@gmail.com

# Index

**A**
American Dream, 118

**B**
Barriers to employability, 97

**C**
Company benefits for hiring reformed offenders, 99
Consumer learner, 112
Contingency plan, 21, 30
Culture, 47, 74–76, 79–80, 82–83

**D**
Data breaches, 19–24, 27–28, 32
Diversity, 73, 78–80, 82–83

**E**
Employee retention, 1–4, 8–9, 11, 43, 47
Environmental protection, 5–6
Equity, 55, 73
Ethical leadership, 39–49
Ethics, 39, 41, 43–45, 47–48

**F**
Fair compensation, 1, 2, 4, 5, 8–11
Front line faculty, 111

**I**
Inclusion, 73–74, 76
Induced fit, 84
Institution, 116–119

**J**
Job satisfaction, 3, 8–9, 44, 48, 101

**L**
Labor shortage, 91, 98, 100–101
Living wage, 4–5, 8–10
Local communities, 2, 7–8

**M**
Marketing, 111–112, 114–115
Mass incarceration, 63–66
Morality, 39, 41, 44

**N**
New dimension, 84
New paradigm, 74
New psychology of leadership, 83

**O**
Organization, 3, 9–10, 22–24, 26, 30–31, 39–41, 43, 45–49, 74, 80–81

**P**
Paradigm shift, 80, 114
Pipeline to prison, 66
Public education, 58–59, 64

**R**
Recidivism, 62–63, 92–94, 96–97, 101
Reformed offenders, 91–101
Remediation costs, 19, 24, 27, 32, 64
Reputational damage, 19, 24, 27, 32

**S**
Small business sustainability, 1–9, 11

**T**
Transformational leadership, 40–42

**U**
U.S. Small Business Administration, 4

**W**
Wage theft, 8, 10–11
White privilege, 75
Workers' rights, 9–10
Workplace safety, 5

# The Refractive Thinker®

## 2023 CATALOG

# The Refractive Thinker®: An Anthology of Higher Learning

### The Refractive Thinker® Press

info@refractivethinker.com
https://RefractiveThinker.com
blog: www.DissertationPublishing.com

*Individual authors own the copyright to their individual materials. The Refractive Thinker® Press has each author's permission to reprint.*

Books are available through The Refractive Thinker® Press at special discounts for bulk purchases for the purpose of sales-promotion, seminar attendance, or educational purposes. Special volumes can be created for specific purposes and to organizational specifications. Orders placed on https://RefractiveThinker.com for students and those in the military receive a 15% discount. Please contact us for further details.

Refractive Thinker® logo by Joey Root; The Refractive Thinker® Press logo design by Jacqueline Teng, cover design by Peri Poloni Gabriel, Knockout Design (knockoutbooks.com), cover design & production by Gary A. Rosenberg (thebookcouple.com).

*I think therefore I am.*
—Renee Descartes

*I critically think to be. I refractively think to change the world.*

Thank you for joining us as we continue to celebrate the accomplishments of doctoral scholars affiliated with many phenomenal institutions of higher learning. The purpose of the anthology series is to share a glimpse into the scholarly works of participating authors on various subjects.

*The Refractive Thinker*® serves the tenets of leadership, which is not simply a concept outside of the self, but comes from within, defining our very essence; where the search to define leadership becomes our personal journey, not yet a finite destination.

*The Refractive Thinker*® is an intimate expression of who we are: the ability to think beyond the traditional boundaries of thinking and critical thinking. Instead of mere reflection and evaluation, one challenges the very boundaries of the constructs itself. If thinking is *inside* the box, and critical thinking is *outside* the box, we add the next step of refractive thinking, *beyond* the box. Perhaps the need exists to dissolve the box completely. The authors within these pages are on a mission to change the world. They are never satisfied or quite content with *what is* or asking *why,* instead these authors intentionally strive to push and test the limits to ask *why not*.

We look forward to your interest in discussing future opportunities. Let our collection of authors continue the journey initiated with Volume I, to which *The Refractive Thinker*® will serve as our guide to future volumes. Come join us in our quest to be refractive thinkers and add your wisdom to the collective. We look forward to your stories.

Please contact *The Refractive Thinker*® Press for information regarding these authors and the works contained within these pages. Perhaps you or your organization may be looking for an author's expertise to incorporate as part of your annual corporate meetings as a keynote or guest speaker(s), perhaps to offer individual, or group seminars or coaching, or require their expertise as consultants.

Join us on our continuing adventures of *The Refractive Thinker*® where we expand the discussion specifically begun in Volume I: Leadership; Volume II (Editions 1–3): Research Methodology; Volume III: Change Management; Volume IV: Ethics, Leadership, and Globalization; Volume V: Strategy in Innovation; Volume VI: Post-Secondary Education; Volume VII: Social Responsibility; Volume VIII: Effective Business Practices in Motivation & Communication; Volume IX: Effective Business Practices in Leadership & Emerging Technologies; Volume X: Effective Business Strategies for the Defense Industry Sector; Volume XI: Women in Leadership; Volume XII: Cybersecurity in an Increasingly Insecure World; Volume XIV: Health Care; Volume XV: Nonprofits; Volume XVI: Generations: Strategies for Managing Generations in the Workforce; Volume XVII: Managing a Cultural Workforce: The Impact of Global Employees; Volume XVIII: Project Management: Strategies to Enhance Workflow & Productivity; Volume XIX: Social Media; Volume XX: Crisis Management; Volume XXI: Work-Life Balance; Volume XXII: Leading Global Conflict; and Volume XXIII: Criminal Justice. All our volumes are themed to explore the realm of strategic thought, creativity, and innovation.

**Dr. Cheryl A. Lentz, managing editor of The Lentz Leadership Institute, explains the unique benefits of the books for readers:**

*"They celebrate the diffusion of innovative refractive thinking through the writings of these doctoral scholars as they dare to think differently in search of new applications and understandings of research. Unlike most academic books that merely define research, The Refractive Thinker® offers unique applications of research from the perspective of multiple authors—each offering a chapter based on their specific expertise."*

# THE REFRACTIVE THINKER® PRESS

*Volume I: An Anthology of Higher Learning*

*Volume II, 1st through 3rd Editions: Research Methodology*

*Volume III: Change Management*

*Volume IV: Ethics, Leadership, and Globalization*

*Volume V: Strategy in Innovation*

*Volume VI: Post-Secondary Education*

*Volume VII: Social Responsibility*

*Volume VIII: Effective Business Practices for Motivation and Communication*

*Volume IX: Effective Business Practices in Leadership & Emerging Technologies*

*Volume X: Effective Business Strategies for the Defense Industry Sector*

*Volume XI: Women in Leadership*

*Volume XII: Cybersecurity in an Increasingly Insecure World*

*Volume XIII: Entrepreneurship: Growing the Future of Business*

*Volume XIV: Health Care: The Impact on Leadership, Business, and Education*

*Volume XV: Nonprofits: Strategies for Effective Management*

*Volume XVI: Generations: Strategies for Managing Generations in the Workforce*

*Volume XVII: Managing a Cultural Workforce: The Impact of Global Employees*

*Volume XVIII: Project Management: Strategies to Enhance Workflow & Productivity*

*Volume XIX: Social Media: Changing the World Through Communication*

*Volume XX: Crisis Management: Effective Business Solutions for Emergency Situations*

*Volume XXI: Work-Life Balance: Effective Strategies to Enhance Success*

*Volume XXII: Leading Global Conflict: Effective Business Solutions in a Post-Pandemic World*

*Volume XXIII: Criminal Justice: Effective Ethical Policies and Practices*

Refractive Thinker volumes are available in e-book, Kindle®, iPad®, Nook®, and Sony Reader™, as well as individual e-chapters by author.

## *Coming Soon from The Refractive Thinker®!*
### AVAILABLE THRU THE LENTZ LEADERSHIP INSTITUTE
### *The Refractive Thinker®: Vol XXIV—Mental Health*

**Telephone orders:** Call us at 702.719.9214

- **Email Orders:** drcheryllentz@gmail.com
- **Website orders:** Please place orders through our website: https://RefractiveThinker.com

## OUR NEWEST RELEASE

### The Refractive Thinker® Volume XXIII: Criminal Justice: Effective Ethical Policies and Practices

Join contributing scholars in their discussions of their doctoral research findings into the ever-changing subject of criminal justice and how existing

practices have been affected by the pandemic. Doctoral scholars share and discuss the latest research regarding what we have learned from the ramifications of the global pandemic. Come join us for one of the most compelling volumes in the Refractive Thinker series.

---

### The Refractive Thinker® Volume XXII: Leading Global Conflict: Effective Business Solutions in a Post-Pandemic World

Join contributing scholars in their discussions of their doctoral research findings into business solutions in an environment forever changed by the ongoing pandemic. Doctoral scholars share current research and words of wisdom regarding what we have learned from this latest crisis, as rapid global changes continue to shape the business landscape. Come join us for one of the most important volumes in the Refractive Thinker series.

---

For more information, please visit our website: **https://RefractiveThinker.com**

#1 INTERNATIONAL BEST SELLER

**The Refractive Thinker® Volume XXI: Work-Life Balance: Effective Strategies to Enhance Personal and Professional Success**

Join contributing scholars in their discussion of their doctoral research findings regarding effective management of personal and professional boundaries in the pursuit of a balanced life. Doctoral scholars share current research and their words of wisdom regarding how to optimize the time spent pursuing business goals versus personal achievements. Are you in the know regarding the most up-to-date and effective time-management strategies in your field of study? Come join us to be part of the conversation of future success in business leadership around the world.

---

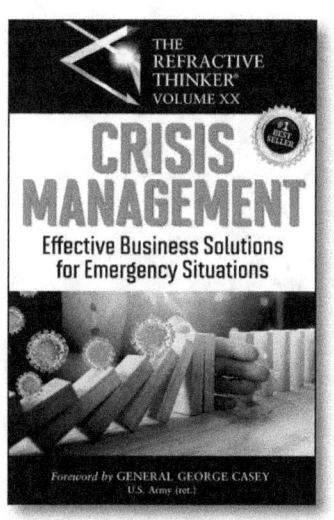

#1 BEST SELLER!

**The Refractive Thinker® Volume XX: Crisis Management: Effective Business Solutions for Emergency Situations**

Join contributing scholars in their discussion of their doctoral research findings regarding effective crisis management strategies. Doctoral scholars share current research and their words of wisdom regarding what we have learned from various crises within the current generation as global discussion continues to shape the business landscape. Are you in the know regarding the most up-to-date and effective strategies in your field of study? Come join us to be part of the conversation of future success in business leadership around the world.

---

For more information, please visit our website: **https://RefractiveThinker.com**

#1 BEST SELLER!

## The Refractive Thinker® Volume XIX: Social Media: Changing the World Through Communication

Join Steve Farber, creator of Extreme Leadership and contributing scholars as they discuss doctoral research findings regarding the importance of social media. Doctoral scholars will share current research and their words of wisdom regarding effective strategies best used within various social media platforms as part of effective global conversations using digital communication. Are you in the know regarding the most up to date and effective strategies? Come join us! This volume will continue to shape the conversation of future success in business leadership around the world.

---

#1 INTERNATIONAL BEST SELLER!

## The Refractive Thinker® Volume XVIII: Project Management: Strategies to Enhance Workflow & Productivity

Join contributing scholars as they discuss doctoral research findings regarding the exciting field of project management. Doctoral scholars share current research and their words of wisdom regarding effective strategies project managers use to enhance workflow and increase productivity. Are you in the know regarding the most up-to-date strategies? Come join us! This volume will continue to shape the conversation of future success in business leadership around the world.

---

For more information, please visit our website: https://RefractiveThinker.com

# PUBLICATIONS ORDER FORM

**Please send the following books from The Refractive Thinker®:**

- ☐ Volume I: An Anthology of Higher Learning
- ☐ Volume II: Research Methodology
- ☐ Volume II: Research Methodology, 2nd Edition
- ☐ Volume II: Research Methodology, 3rd Edition
- ☐ Volume III: Change Management
- ☐ Volume IV: Ethics, Leadership, and Globalization
- ☐ Volume V: Strategy in Innovation
- ☐ Volume VI: Post-Secondary Education
- ☐ Volume VII: Social Responsibility
- ☐ Volume VIII: Effective Business Practices
- ☐ Volume IX: Effective Business Practices in Leadership & Emerging Technologies
- ☐ Volume X: Effective Business Strategies for the Defense Industry Sector
- ☐ Volume XI: Women in Leadership
- ☐ Volume XII: Cybersecurity
- ☐ Volume XIII: Entrepreneurship
- ☐ Volume XIV: Health care
- ☐ Volume XV: Nonprofits
- ☐ Volume XVI: Generations
- ☐ Volume XVII: Managing a Cultural Workforce
- ☐ Volume XVIII: Project Management
- ☐ Volume XIX: Social Media
- ☐ Volume XX: Crisis Management
- ☐ Volume XXI: Work-Life Balance
- ☐ Volume XXII: Leading Global Conflict
- ☐ Volume XXIII: Criminal Justice

Please contact the Refractive Thinker® Press for book prices, e-book prices, and shipping. Individual e-chapters available by author: $3.95 (plus applicable tax).   https://RefractiveThinker.com

- ☐ So You Think You Can Edit?
- ☐ The Expert Success Solution
- ☐ The Unbounded Dimensions Series
- ☐ Ethics, Employment Law, and Faith-Based Universities
- ☐ Effective Study Skills in 5 Simple Steps
- ☐ Technology That Tutors
- ☐ Siberian Husky Rescue
- ☐ The Consumer Learner
- ☐ Journey Outside the Golden Palace
- ☐ The Dissertation Toolbox

**Please send more FREE information:**

☐ Speaking engagements    ☐ Educational seminars    ☐ Consulting

**Join our mailing list:**

Name: _____

Address: _____

City: _____  State: _____  Zip: _____

Telephone: _____  Email: _____

# Participation in Future Volumes of The Refractive Thinker®

Yes, I would like to participate in:

❑ **Doctoral Volume**(s) for a specific university or organization:

Name: _____

Contact Person: _____

Telephone: _____ E-mail: _____


❑ **Specialized Volume**(s) Business or Themed:

Name: _____

Contact Person: _____

Telephone: _____ E-mail: _____


E-mail form to:     The Refractive Thinker® Press
drcheryllentz@gmail.com
https://RefractiveThinker.com

## Join us on Twitter, LinkedIn, and Facebook

www.ingramcontent.com/pod-product-compliance
Lightning Source LLC
Chambersburg PA
CBHW071456080526
44587CB00014B/2127